Israel Chukwuka Okunwaye

PRAYER INTELLIGENCE:

On Conversation with the Invisible Creator Being of the Universe- Finding a Biblical Basis?

A response to billions of people who pray and desire to do so better,

with reference to scriptural principles of Christian prayer.

On Rights and Permissions

Author/Publisher, ©Israel Chukwuka Okunwaye, 2020.

For all correspondence, address to-

    27 Old Gloucester Street, London
    WC1N 3AX
    United Kingdom
    or, Email: write@israelokunwaye.com

Printed by *CreateSpace*- KDP, an Amazon.com Company. Available on Kindle and other retail outlets.

Israel Chukwuka Okunwaye has asserted all his rights under the Copyright, Designs and Patents Act, 1998, to be identified as Author of this work.

All rights reserved.

No part of this publication may be reproduced, stored in a retrieval system, or transmitted, in any form or by any means, electronic, mechanical, photocopying, recording or otherwise be copied for public or private use, other than for 'fair use' as brief quotations embodied in articles and reviews, without the prior written permission of the Author/Publisher, or as expressly permitted by law.

Unless otherwise stated, Scripture quotations [from the specified version and passage references] in this publication are from the Holy Bible. All rights reserved.

First published 2020

British Library Cataloguing in Publication Data: a catalogue record for this book is available from the British Library.

ISBN: 978-1-9164445-6-0 (Paperback); 978-1-9164445-7-7 (KDP)

www.israelokunwaye.com
www.glyglobal.com
GLYGLOBAL®

Dedication

My thanks to the living God, Creator of the heavens and the earth, and Father of our Lord Jesus Christ of Nazareth, for His love, grace, glory, wisdom, and greatness.

To those who pray and look to God for their daily sustenance and entrust to Him the keeping of their souls.

To those who believed they received answers to their prayers after no possible means of human intervention, and to those who felt astonishing and unprecedented help only came through others after they prayed to God.

To you who bought this book with the intention to develop your idea on prayer.

Preface

I am glad to complete this manuscript on prayer and present it to you. I hope you find my thoughts helpful in your walk with God, as you develop the intimate art of conversation with an invisible being who happen to be the creator of the universe - Jesus shows us how to do this.

These 33 chapters on prayer, is my attempt to be exhaustive on the subject, but I know God may show you more. I have found His leadership on this study and writing most thrilling, and I was amazed at what I found. Developing conversation with the living God is a priviledge. And thank God it is no fables, as Christ has practically made God known. It is my prayer this enriches your experience. This work is very reliant on Christian scripture.

This is my fourth book. Up to this time, I have never felt as sapped of strength writing a book as I did this one, and I think I have never prayed more as I did this one - fitting for the title, which is on prayer. I am glad and refreshed this also adopted its unique style, and that I have utmost a sense of peace of work done.

If you struggle with the concept of God, I honestly would for a starter refer you to my book - Authentic Faith.

Enjoy your read with spiritual focus, you will be glad you did! Please let me know how it blessed you. Once again, hope you find this a great resource.

Thanks.

Evangelist. Israel Chukwuka Okunwaye

(Author, & Christian Speaker)

Content

- I. TITLE PAGE
- II. DEDICATION
- III. PREFACE
- IV. INTRODUCTION
- V. CHAPTERS

1. Why Pray?
2. Thy Kingdom Come
3. Faith to Pray
4. Praying in Faith
5. In Christ's Authority
6. The prayer of five men and five women in the scriptures
7. Prayer of the persecuted Church
8. Prayer for spiritual fire (revival)
9. Watch one hour? – 'ought-ness' of prayer
10. Watch and pray
11. Manners of prayer
12. Response to answers in appreciation
13. Humility in prayer, righteousness, the peace of God
14. Postures and voice in prayers, before and after
15. Heaven's discretion
16. Heart and mouth, ear and eyes in prayer

17. Talking to God not man: conversations in prayer
18. tears and joys of perseverance
19. Waiting time
20. Expectations to receive
21. Learning the act of prayer
22. Consider seven points of prayer: Healing, Favour and creativity for honest gain, power to reap and fulfil destiny, protection, family and society, spiritual graces, influence
23. Unified Congregational prayer
24. A consecrated place of prayer - the potency
25. The secret place of prayer
26. The open place of prayer
27. The memorable place of prayer
28. The actions of prayer
29. Prayer and obedience
30. Discerning counterfeit answers and counterfeit prayers, and binding a critic-hypocritical and envious spirit
31. The spirit of prayer, and the joy of fellowship with the Holy Spirit
32. Praying the Scriptures
33. Higher dimensions of prayer: heaven's pre-emptive grace
VI. AUTHOR'S BIOGRAPHY PAGE

Introduction

Much conversation exists on the relationality of prayer but rather diminishing voices on the actuality of prayer. A step that perhaps needs to be expanded and concretised- the embracing of prayer, than what prayer can materially do for you, the internal conflicts, individual experiences and culture, the therapeutic and institutional utilisation, the psychoanalysis and the subtle snobbery of the choice. The canvassing of the philosophy of embracing of prayer in society as a wasteful endeavour, an essential mere mutterings to an imagined or perceived supreme deity of which there could be many, asking him to take control of whatever occasion, is a slippery slope as it suffers from a restrictive classification- because for many prayer means more and it is a core element of their life. Commendable that in society rights to pray are recognised (not impeded by ever changing social norms and growing legislative improvements in their respective domestic regions), and that several governments now think it a worthy example for people to emulate this practice than being obsessed in a self-culture war, which may foster a chronic loss of moral restraint or mutual respect for others, or disrupt some balance or offend some being or alien somewhere in the cosmos for which they don't understand or prepared to test or find; that in itself does the call to prayer no good than shuffling it into a reductionist agenda and one for ritualised celebrations at opening and closing ceremony in unestablished but muted reverence, but truly void of the joyful respect for and soul of prayer, which the bible represents and sets conditions. Prayer has principles, a recipient- that is a person in focus, a heart root, a scriptural foundation, and it may shock you to realise it can be done wrongly. Prayers may need more depth, flowing from a place of understanding. Prayer is communing with God in faith and listening for His response. Several opinions in our common parlance on the ambits of understanding of purpose prayer should not remove the spiritual angle and reverence for Christ. It is not enough to mourn a loss, or whisper keep praying to mean an endless wait, or only something done before diving into a meal with mindless pleasant recitation- it can be more. As a person with individual responsibility and possibilities for influence, your standing on this truth of worship of God is more critical, than seeking to tick a box of compliance.

So, revisiting the biblical pattern I believe would equip with best practices and enable a conversation with God, where you are able to talk in a way consistent with His will and receive answers, and even explore further on what you hear as God permits. In thirty three chapters I expatiate aspects of prayers that could enhance your experience of communing- for instance, the biblical objective of prayer; what Christ means when He talks about bringing God's kingdom reign; what faith has got to do with spiritual biblical Christian meditation or prayer; using Christ's authority; examples of people who prayed in the bible across genders; how to pray in certain times if political turbulence or Christian suffering; need to ask for spiritual strength and sight; understanding the different types of prayer; on humility and thanksgiving in prayer; dealing with what posture or voicing to adopt; on whether God has a discretion; the place of heart and keeping God in focus; on adjusting to God's timing and resilience; also how to manage expectations; having to admit you need to learn to pray and some suggested areas, also on praying with other believers; and I will add- does praying need a private or open location, a memory, designated or pragmatic actions, an instructive book?, and on the work of the Holy Spirit to discern and enable fellowship. I end the 33 sections long work on a reminder to consider using the scripture as a guide in some of your prayers, as it ministers to you, and also then rest in God's goodness, of the one who has all knowledge and ability to work in unlimited ways in your favour. My approach is to be very reliant on biblical scripture to discuss Christian prayer. You will find versions referenced similar in meaning but which I perceive either simpler or best explanatory, and which captures the events or testimonies succinctly. I recommend also checking yourself. I try to avoid too much paraphrasing, if it would leave room for doubt- best to see and read for yourself what God is calling us to. A bit time consuming, but worth it in the end. I use the NKJV, NIV and several more of recommended biblical scriptural text (and I also found online resources as e-Sword, Bible Hub, Bible Study Tools- helpful in this regard) to accomplish this, and on highlighting and explaining the principles of prayer. I endeavour commentaries as necessary and share my admonishing on adopting these God-given principles in your praxis.

Rather than exploring prayer as just a social phenomenon, and cherishing its feel good effect- which thankfully has been suggested in some places could be an outcome, how about exploring further theological truths on the God of prayer and His guiding format and contemplations, and then begin to personally (and alongside other believers of Jesus Christ) enjoy conversations with Him- not just reading about Him. I would recommend you get ready to search the scriptures and leave opportunity to pray as need arise. You would need the help of the Holy Spirit embarking on this route to cracking some tough nut, and opening your heart to do good. Above all, just enjoy the peace, reverence, beauty, and joy, of spending time with God.

Chapters 1-33

Chapter One

WHY PRAY?

- God calls us to pray as a divine instruction.
- God desires that the righteous by faith call out in prayer to Him because He delights in the prayers of the godly.
- It is needful spiritually for fellowship, to converse with God and for our relationship with God to be enhanced.
- Prayer illustrates the blessedness of humility and dependency on God.
- As a response to revelation.
- It is a joy to have conversations with the Father God in heaven.

If there was ever one of many important things to know of God, is that His instructions are life giving. Many a times when He instructed people to take a path, it has often arisen that He has foreseen a situation that might spring a difficulty and spoken to avert it. Those to whom He speaks, do well then to listen. An instruction to prayer is to unlock the potential for great safety mechanism. So, prayer then shifts from a laisse faire movement to one of structured and vital importance, hard necked in, as a matter of importance. Prayer is contingent to survival in this world. You should either be praying, or someone is praying for you- to be completely bereft of prayer is spiritually risky. Every second of our life is held by the grace of God, and we must cry out to God for more grace, and for His work through us to continue unhindered.

Your prayer to God is an offering, the fruit of your lips.

1 Peter 2:5 (NLT), "And you are living stones that God is building into his spiritual temple. What's more, you are his holy priests. Through the mediation of Jesus Christ, you offer spiritual sacrifices that please God."

Hebrews 13:15 (GNT), "Let us, then, always offer praise to God as our sacrifice through Jesus, which is the offering presented by lips that confess him as Lord."

Psalm 141:2 (KJV), "Let my prayer be set forth before thee as incense; and the lifting up of my hands as the evening sacrifice."

Hosea 14:2 (KJV), "Take with you words, and turn to the LORD: say unto him, Take away all iniquity, and receive us graciously: so will we render the calves of our lips."

There is a relationship between the prayers a believer makes and the temple. First there is the temple of the Lord, a consecrated building set apart for prayer to God, but also, we must be in recognition that our body is the temple of the Lord. We may choose to go to the house of the Lord to pray, we can also call out to God from God's holy temple which is in us who fear the Lord. How precious is it, as temples of the Lord revere the Lord in His temple- it is like flames within a fire, all one, none apart! God has a relationship with His temple, His presence is there, there is a part of God that resides there because His name is there. There is a connection God has with us when His Spirit is in us by His grace, it becomes wholesome to be joined to the Lord because His presence quickens our soul and gives life to the spiritually dead.

Jonah 2:7 (GWT), "As my life was slipping away, I remembered the LORD. My prayer came to you in your holy temple."

Romans 9:25-27 [28-33] (NIV), "As he says in Hosea: "I will call them 'my people' who are not my people; and I will call her 'my loved one' who is not my loved one," and, "In the very place where it was said to them, 'You are not my people,' there they will be called 'children of the living God.'"

2 Samuel 7:27-29 (NIV), King David prayed "Lord Almighty, God of Israel, you have revealed this to your servant, saying, 'I will build a house for you.' So your servant has found courage to pray this prayer to you. Sovereign Lord, you are God! Your covenant is trustworthy, and you have promised these good things to your servant. Now be pleased to bless the house of your servant, that it may continue forever in your sight; for you, Sovereign Lord, have spoken, and with your blessing the house of your servant will be blessed forever."

Psalm 4:3-5 (CEV), "The Lord has chosen everyone who is faithful to be his very own, and he answers my prayers. But each of you had better tremble and turn from your sins. Silently search your heart as you lie in bed. Offer the proper sacrifices and trust the Lord."

1 Kings 8:22-30 [31-54] (NKJV), "Then Solomon stood before the altar of the Lord in the presence of all the assembly of Israel, and spread out his hands toward heaven; and he said: "Lord God of Israel, there is no God in heaven above or on earth below like You, who keep Your covenant and mercy with Your servants who walk before You with all their hearts. You have kept what You promised Your servant David my father; You have both spoken with Your mouth and fulfilled it with Your hand, as it is this day. Therefore, Lord God of Israel, now keep what You promised Your servant David my father, saying, 'You shall not fail to have a man sit before Me on the throne of Israel, only if your sons take heed to their way, that they walk before Me as you have walked before Me.' And now I pray, O God of Israel, let Your word come true, which You have spoken to Your servant David my father. "But will God indeed dwell on the earth? Behold, heaven and the heaven of heavens cannot contain You. How

much less this temple which I have built! Yet regard the prayer of Your servant and his supplication, O Lord my God, and listen to the cry and the prayer which Your servant is praying before You today: that Your eyes may be open toward this temple night and day, toward the place of which You said, 'My name shall be there,' that You may hear the prayer which Your servant makes toward this place. And may You hear the supplication of Your servant and of Your people Israel, when they pray toward this place. Hear in heaven Your dwelling place; and when You hear, forgive."

2 Chronicles 7:14 (KJV), "If my people, which are called by my name, shall humble themselves, and pray, and seek my face, and turn from their wicked ways; then will I hear from heaven, and will forgive their sin, and will heal their land."

Psalm 34:4-6 (NLT), "I prayed to the LORD, and he answered me. He freed me from all my fears. Those who look to him for help will be radiant with joy; no shadow of shame will darken their faces. In my desperation I prayed, and the LORD listened; he saved me from all my troubles."

Prayers can be made from the temple of the Lord for healing, healing of the body, soul and mind.

2 Kings 20: 1-11 (NLT), "About that time Hezekiah became deathly ill, and the prophet Isaiah son of Amoz went to visit him. He gave the king this message: "This is what the LORD says: Set your affairs in order, for you are going to die. You will not recover from this illness."

When Hezekiah heard this, he turned his face to the wall and prayed to the LORD, "Remember, O LORD, how I have always been faithful to you and have served you single-mindedly, always doing what pleases you." Then he broke down and wept bitterly. But before Isaiah had left the middle courtyard, this message came to him from the LORD: "Go back to Hezekiah, the leader of my people. Tell him, 'This is what the LORD, the God of your ancestor David, says: I have heard your prayer and seen your tears. I will heal you, and three days from now you will get out of bed and go to the Temple of the LORD. I will add fifteen years to your life, and I will rescue you and this city from the king of Assyria. I will defend this city for my own honor and for the sake of my servant David.'"

Then Isaiah said, "Make an ointment from figs." So Hezekiah's servants spread the ointment over the boil, and Hezekiah recovered! Meanwhile, Hezekiah had said to Isaiah, "What sign will the LORD give to prove that he will heal me and that I will go to the Temple of the LORD three days from now?"

Isaiah replied, "This is the sign from the LORD to prove that he will do as he promised. Would you like the shadow on the sundial to go forward ten steps or backward ten steps?" "The shadow always moves forward," Hezekiah replied, "so that would be easy. Make it go ten steps backward instead." So Isaiah the prophet asked the LORD to do this, and he caused the shadow to move ten steps backward on the sundial of Ahaz!"

Nehemiah 1:6 (GNT), "Look at me, LORD, and hear my prayer, as I pray day and night for your servants, the people of Israel. I confess that we, the people of Israel, have sinned. My ancestors and I have sinned."

Psalm 65:2 (ESV), "O you who hear prayer, to you shall all flesh come."

Matthew 17:14-21 (WNT), "When they had returned to the people, there came to Him a man who fell on his knees before Him and besought Him. "Sir," he said, "have pity on my son, for he is an epileptic and is very ill. Often he falls into the fire and often into the water. I have brought him to your disciples, and they have not been able to cure him." "O unbelieving and perverse generation!" replied Jesus; "how long shall I be with you? how long shall I endure you? Bring him to me." Then Jesus reprimanded the demon, and it came out and left him; and the boy was cured from that moment. Then the disciples came to Jesus privately and asked Him, "Why could not we expel the demon?" "Because your faith is so small," He replied; "for I solemnly declare to you that if you have faith like a mustard-seed, you shall say to this mountain, 'Remove from this place to that,' and it will remove; and nothing shall be impossible to you. But an evil spirit of this kind is only driven out by prayer and fasting."

The call to prayer is serious work and requires devotion. Rather than be perturbed and divided- it is better to pray.

Acts 6: 1-7 (NLT), "But as the believers rapidly multiplied, there were rumblings of discontent. The Greek-speaking believers complained about the Hebrew-speaking believers, saying that their widows were being discriminated against in the daily distribution of food. So the Twelve called a meeting of all the believers. They said, "We apostles should spend our time teaching the word of God, not running a food program. And so, brothers, select seven men who are well respected and are full of the Spirit and wisdom. We will give them this responsibility. Then we apostles can spend our time in prayer and teaching the word." Everyone liked this idea, and they chose the following: Stephen (a man full of faith and the Holy Spirit), Philip, Procorus, Nicanor, Timon, Parmenas, and Nicolas of Antioch (an earlier convert to the Jewish faith). These seven were presented to the apostles, who prayed for them as they laid their hands on them. So God's message continued to spread. The number of believers greatly increased in Jerusalem, and many of the Jewish priests were converted, too."

Philippians 4:6 (CEV), "Don't worry about anything, but pray about everything. With thankful hearts offer up your prayers and requests to God."

1 Timothy 4:1-5 (GNT), "The Spirit says clearly that some people will abandon the faith in later times; they will obey lying spirits and follow the teachings of demons. Such teachings are spread by deceitful liars, whose consciences are dead, as if burnt with a hot iron. Such people teach that it is wrong to marry and to eat certain foods. But God created those foods to be eaten, after a prayer of thanks, by those who are believers and have come to know the truth. Everything that God has created is good; nothing is to be rejected, but everything is to be received with a prayer of thanks, because the word of God and the prayer make it acceptable to God."

James 5:13-18 (NASB), "Is anyone among you suffering? Let him pray. Is anyone cheerful? Let him sing praises. Is anyone among you sick? Let him call for the elders of the church, and let them pray over him, anointing him with oil in the name of the Lord; and the prayer offered in faith will restore the one who is sick, and the Lord will raise him up, and if he has committed sins, they will be forgiven him. Therefore, confess your sins to one another, and pray for one another, so that you may be healed. The effective prayer of a righteous man can accomplish much. Elijah was a man with a nature like ours, and he prayed earnestly that it might not rain; and it did not rain on the earth for three years and six months. And he prayed again, and the sky poured rain, and the earth produced its fruit."

Praying is an opportunity to come into spiritual maturity.

Colossians 4:12 (ESV), "Epaphras, who is one of you, a servant of Christ Jesus, greets you, always struggling on your behalf in his prayers, that you may stand mature and fully assured in all the will of God."

Matthew 9:38 (NLT), "Jesus traveled through all the towns and villages of that area, teaching in the synagogues and announcing the Good News about the Kingdom. And he healed every kind of disease and illness. When he saw the crowds, he had compassion on them because they were confused and helpless, like sheep without a shepherd. He said to his disciples, "The harvest is great, but the workers are few. So pray to the Lord who is in charge of the harvest; ask him to send more workers into his fields.""

2 Thessalonians 3:1-2 [5] (KJV), "Finally, brethren, pray for us, that the word of the Lord may have free course, and be glorified, even as it is with you: And that we may be delivered from unreasonable and wicked men: for all men have not faith."

Job 21:15-16 (NIV), "Who is the Almighty, that we should serve him? What would we gain by praying to him?' But their prosperity is not in their own hands, so I stand aloof from the plans of the wicked."

Colossians 4:2-4 (GWT), "Keep praying. Pay attention when you offer prayers of thanksgiving. At the same time also pray for us. Pray that God will give us an opportunity to speak the word so that we may tell the mystery about Christ. It is because of this mystery that I am a prisoner.

Pray that I may make this mystery as clear as possible. This is what I have to do."

Zechariah 4:6 (GNB), "The angel told me to give Zerubbabel this message from the LORD: "You will succeed, not by military might or by your own strength, but by my spirit."

THY KINGDOM COME

- It is important we insist God's principles is enthroned on the earth. This is our spiritual worship.

- It is about building God's spiritual kingdom.

- There is a connection between the sovereign power of God in heaven and His influence on earth, as He wills.

- Also, the prayer we make on earth can create a heavenly response of grace.

In Luke 11:2 (NLT), "Jesus said, "This is how you should pray: "Father, may your name be kept holy. May your Kingdom come soon.""

The Psalmist shows us how to extol the Lord-

Psalm 92:4 (NKJV), "For You, LORD, have made me glad through Your work; I will triumph in the works of Your hands."

Psalm 93:1-5 (NKJV), "The LORD reigns, He is clothed with majesty;
The LORD has clothed and girded Himself with strength;
Indeed, the world is firmly established, it will not be moved.

Your throne is established from of old;
You are from everlasting.
The floods have lifted up, O LORD,
The floods have lifted up their voice,
The floods lift up their pounding waves.
More than the sounds of many waters,
Than the mighty breakers of the sea,
The LORD on high is mighty.
Your testimonies are fully confirmed;
Holiness befits Your house,
O LORD, forevermore."

Psalm 102:12-22 (NKJV), "But you, O LORD, remain forever. You are remembered throughout every generation. You will rise and have compassion on Zion, because it is time to grant a favor to it. Indeed, the appointed time has come. Your servants value Zion's stones, and they pity its rubble. The nations will fear the LORD's name. All the kings of the earth will fear your glory. When the LORD builds Zion, he will appear in his glory. He will turn his attention to the prayers of those who have been abandoned. He will not despise their prayers. This will be written down for a future generation so that a people yet to be created may praise the LORD: "The LORD looked down from his holy place high above. From heaven he looked at the earth. He heard the groans of the prisoners and set free those who were condemned to death. The LORD's name is announced in Zion and his praise in Jerusalem when nations and kingdoms gather to worship the LORD."

Also consider God does not take likely to the fact His name is brought to disrepute, by not hallowing His name as holy. We do this when God is made to compete for His place with other gods, rather than serving Him only and wholly. Also, God is brought to disrepute when we disregard His word and speak of God as inconsequential or vain. God loves you, and is concerned about how you as part of His body, His people, can continually keep growing and be more like Him. He protects us with a godly jealously and wants us to not focus on self, but ask for His strength and will, to reign, as from above. Consider these scriptures, that highlights His will for His people.

Amos 5:18-27 (GWT), "How horrible it will be for those who long for the day of the LORD! Why do you long for that day? The day of the LORD is one of darkness and not light. It is like a person who flees from a lion only to be attacked by a bear. It is like a person who goes home and puts his hand on the wall only to be bitten by a snake.

The day of the LORD brings darkness and not light. It is pitch black, with no light. I hate your festivals; I despise them. I'm not pleased with your religious assemblies. Even though you bring me burnt offerings and grain offerings, I won't accept them. I won't even look at the fellowship offerings of your choicest animals. Spare me the sound of your songs. I won't listen to the music of your harps.

But let justice flow like a river and righteousness like an ever-flowing stream. Did you bring me sacrifices and grain offerings in the desert for 40 years, nation of Israel? You carried along the statues of [the god] Sikkuth as your king and the star Kiyyun, the gods you made for yourselves. I will send you into exile beyond Damascus, says the LORD, whose name is the God of Armies."

Psalm 92:9-15 (ESV), "For behold, your enemies, O Lord, for behold, your enemies shall perish; all evildoers shall be scattered. But you have exalted my horn like that of the wild ox; you have poured over me fresh oil. My eyes have seen the downfall of my enemies; my ears have heard the doom of my evil assailants. The righteous flourish like the palm tree and grow like a cedar in Lebanon. They are planted in the house of the Lord; they flourish in the courts of our God. They still bear fruit in old age; they are ever full of sap and green, to declare that the Lord is upright; he is my rock, and there is no unrighteousness in him."

Luke 22:39-44 (NIV), "Jesus went out as usual to the Mount of Olives, and his disciples followed him. On reaching the place, he said to them, "Pray that you will not fall into temptation." He withdrew about a stone's throw beyond them, knelt down and prayed, "Father, if you are willing, take this cup from me; yet not my will, but yours be done." An angel from heaven appeared to him and strengthened him. And being in anguish, he prayed more earnestly, and his sweat was like drops of blood falling to the ground."

2 Chronicles 7:14 (NIV), "if my people, who are called by my name, will humble themselves and pray and seek my face and turn from their wicked ways, then I will hear from heaven, and I will forgive their sin and will heal their land."

Jonah 4:1-10 (NLT), "This change of plans greatly upset Jonah, and he became very angry. So he complained to the LORD about it: "Didn't I say before I left home that you would do this, LORD? That is why I ran away to Tarshish! I knew that you are a merciful and compassionate God, slow to get angry and filled with unfailing love. You are eager to turn back from destroying people. Just kill me now, LORD! I'd rather be dead than alive if what I predicted will not happen."

The LORD replied, "Is it right for you to be angry about this?"

Then Jonah went out to the east side of the city and made a shelter to sit under as he waited to see what would happen to the city. And the LORD God arranged for a leafy plant to grow there, and soon it spread its broad leaves over Jonah's head, shading him from the sun. This eased his discomfort, and Jonah was very grateful for the plant.

But God also arranged for a worm! The next morning at dawn the worm ate through the stem of the plant so that it withered away. And as the sun grew hot, God arranged for a scorching east wind to blow on Jonah. The sun beat down on his head until he grew faint and wished to die. "Death is certainly better than living like this!" he exclaimed.

Then God said to Jonah, "Is it right for you to be angry because the plant died?"

"Yes," Jonah retorted, "even angry enough to die!"

Then the LORD said, "You feel sorry about the plant, though you did nothing to put it there. It came quickly and died quickly. But Nineveh has more than 120,000 people living in spiritual darkness, not to mention all the animals. Shouldn't I feel sorry for such a great city?' "

Hebrew 2:14 (GWT), "Since all of these sons and daughters have flesh and blood, Jesus took on flesh and blood to be like them. He did this so that by dying he would destroy the one who had power over death (that is, the devil)."

John 16:13 (NIV), "But when he, the Spirit of truth, comes, he will guide you into all the truth. He will not speak on his own; he will speak only what he hears, and he will tell you what is yet to come."

Acts 4:32 (NKJV), "Now the multitude of those who believed were of one heart and one soul; neither did anyone say that any of the things he possessed was his own, but they had all things in common."

1 Corinthians 3:6-9 (NAS), "I planted, Apollos watered, but God was causing the growth. So then neither the one who plants nor the one who waters is anything, but God who causes the growth. Now he who plants and he who waters are one; but each will receive his own reward according to his own labor. For we are God's fellow workers; you are God's field, God's building."

Chapter Three

FAITH TO PRAY

- There is a place to say, grant us faith oh Lord.
- One can operate from the place of believing that God is able to do what we ask.
- In that place of knowledge, we are able to come to communion with the Father.
- Also, there is need to stir up your faith as a believer, to pray. If you are weak in faith you would feel no urgency for prayer when need arises.
- Remember, whatever is not of faith is sin, therefore prayer must be from a place of faith, but it is only when you are of faith you can genuinely pray.

When your heart is overwhelmed and is fainting, and you lack courage or words to say, or the ability to do anything, God's spirit can impart faith into you and stir you up to pray. It's like a sweet perfume that triggers the brain to react to the fragrance and lighten a mood, it's like the taste of honey on a child's tongue that could cause a burst of dances- faith energises you to respond to God. You cannot pray by yourself you need

God. His prompt, His strength, His grace. Yes, you maybe downcast, but how God's outstretched hands lift us up to come talk to Him. It is as if you see the Father say come, talk to me.

Galatians 4:6 (NLT) (Romans 8:15), "And because we are his children, God has sent the Spirit of his Son into our hearts, prompting us to call out, "Abba, Father.""

2 Kings 2:11-15 GNT, "They kept talking as they walked on; then suddenly a chariot of fire pulled by horses of fire came between them, and Elijah was taken up to heaven by a whirlwind. Elisha saw it and cried out to Elijah, "My father, my father! Mighty defender of Israel! You are gone!" And he never saw Elijah again. In grief Elisha tore his cloak in two. Then he picked up Elijah's cloak that had fallen from him, and went back and stood on the bank of the Jordan. 14He struck the water with Elijah's cloak and said, "Where is the Lord, the God of Elijah?" Then he struck the water again, and it divided, and he walked over to the other side. The fifty prophets from Jericho saw him and said, "The power of Elijah is on Elisha!" They went to meet him, bowed down before him"

Zechariah 4:6 (CEV), "So the angel explained that it was the following message of the LORD to Zerubbabel: I am the LORD All-Powerful. So don't depend on your own power or strength, but on my Spirit."

Isaiah 40 :25-31 (NKJV), "Have you not known? Have you not heard?
The everlasting God, the Lord,
The Creator of the ends of the earth,
Neither faints nor is weary.
His understanding is unsearchable.
He gives power to the weak,
And to those who have no might He increases strength.
Even the youths shall faint and be weary,
And the young men shall utterly fall,
But those who wait on the Lord
Shall renew their strength;

They shall mount up with wings like eagles,
They shall run and not be weary,
They shall walk and not faint."

John 15:5 (GWT), ""'I am the vine. You are the branches. Those who live in me while I live in them will produce a lot of fruit. But you can't produce anything without me."

Prophet Daniel had an experience with a divine being who gave him strength for conversation-

Daniel 10:18-19 (NLT), "Then the one who looked like a man touched me again, and I felt my strength returning. "Don't be afraid," he said, "for you are very precious to God. Peace! Be encouraged! Be strong!"

As he spoke these words to me, I suddenly felt stronger and said to him, "Please speak to me, my lord, for you have strengthened me.""

Jesus needed the strength from God's Spirit in the moments of His suffering-

Luke 22:41-44 (GNT), "Then he went off from them about the distance of a stone's throw and knelt down and prayed. "Father," he said, "if you will, take this cup of suffering away from me. Not my will, however, but your will be done." An angel from heaven appeared to him and strengthened him. In great anguish he prayed even more fervently; his sweat was like drops of blood falling to the ground."

Our prayers are not as effective if all dependent on the flesh. It is dry and lacking depth. Samson would soon realise He needed God, when he jumped in his strength.

Judges 16:20 (NLT), "Then she cried out, "Samson! The Philistines have come to capture you!" When he woke up, he thought, "I will do as before and shake myself free." But he didn't realize the LORD had left him."

Like the Apostles, we can ask for more grace.

Luke 17:5 (NKJV), "And the apostles said to the Lord, "Increase our faith.""

Chapter Four

PRAYING IN FAITH

- To start is one thing, to continue is another. Praying in faith is about sustainability.

- I distinguish between faith to pray, and praying in faith. The first is positional and the second is in response to a situation. The believer of Christ has been placed in right standing with God, so has received grace from His Spirit, he or she already has a believing faith in their heart, so are able to speak to God as Father. That ability is faith to pray. God imparts this faith to those who genuine seek after the true God. Christ brings this dimension of God to us, showing us the Father. Many in their search for God have come to access this by unspeakable grace and gift of God- I may reference Cornelius finding favour with God, and being drawn towards relationship. Or of Moses hearing a call from God pulling him towards God revealed in a holy fire. Through Christ's work we are impacted with faith from God and are able to begin communing with Him, from the position of a relationship. However, praying in faith comes from increasing knowledge, the more you come to know about God gives you impetus to place a demand and deepens the level you can exercise your faith.

- This is a kind of prayer done when you pray believing God is able to do all things. For some believers in some situation can pray in faith, whilst some cannot pray in faith in that similar situation- some can believe God to supply bread but not raise the dead. Each man to his measure of faith. Others can say if the Lord wills He can.

- You really shouldn't be praying if you don't trust God hears, and can respond- no point persistently dissing God. However, do not pray, asking wrongly, not knowing the heart of God in a situation per time, some doors might need to stay closed, whilst some doors may need to open that has been shut. It is God that can open or shut a door.

- An Abraham case study shows us a level of faith that continues to work in his absence. He prayed, blessing his descendants leaving them with inheritances and godly instruction, trusting that when he died God was able to sustain what they had received and increase them. He believed God continually in life, and we see the effect continually in death. Concerning Isaac, Abraham prayed a blessing, similarly Jacob received a blessing from Isaac his father and then Jacob blessed his sons. Even in difficulty the blessing prayer produced grace. Genesis 25:5-6; Proverbs 13:22; Genesis 22:17; Hebrews 11:17-21.

- Also, Luke 7:1-10 case study: There are clues we see, a verbal request, tears, silent action, and also a continuing working of faith by prayer. Jesus in responded to the Centurion's plea (via his friends) to minister to his employee who was ill in his house (and mentioned Christ didn't need to come but speak a word). Christ granted his wish, and we see God respond to an active faith, acting in Christ's absence, irrespective of distance and time. Both the man's prayer in request and Christ's prayer of healing, both unwavering and constant produces God's healing power. Though the one sick, in that state was being interceded for, perhaps not in a state to speak and weak, there was grace available working over time, place, distance. Concerning Abraham we see an unwavering faith stretch over a generation, with the Centurion we see his faith extend to another in his house, those who delivered his request to Jesus returned to find him waiting in anticipation and the found the servant healed. Christ saw his faith, even though he saw in humility his unworthiness for the Lord to come visiting- truly Christ's word is enough. The Lord is not bodily with us, but thanks be to God He left us His word. So, we pray expecting His will to be done.

Consider this, whatever we do has to be done in faith- even praying, so it's not reduced to just soliloquising. Expect an answer from God as you talk to God, though He is physically absent, He is however present in with you in Spirit and hears. Do your prayers this way, and let your actions reflect this confidence, and stay on it. See these scriptures-

In Romans 14:22-23 (ESV), "The faith that you have, keep between yourself and God. Blessed is the one who has no reason to pass judgment on himself for what he approves. But whoever has doubts is condemned if he eats, because the eating is not from faith. For whatever does not proceed from faith is sin"

Psalm 5:2-3 (ISV), "Pay attention to my cry for help, my king and my God, for unto you will I pray. LORD, in the morning you will hear my voice; in the morning I will pray to you, and I will watch for your answer."

Matthew 21:18-22 (NLT), "In the morning, as Jesus was returning to Jerusalem, he was hungry, and he noticed a fig tree beside the road. He went over to see if there were any figs, but there were only leaves. Then he said to it, "May you never bear fruit again!" And immediately the fig tree withered up. The disciples were amazed when they saw this and asked, "How did the fig tree wither so quickly?" Then Jesus told them, "I tell you the truth, if you have faith and don't doubt, you can do things like this and much more. You can even say to this mountain, 'May you be lifted up and thrown into the sea,' and it will happen. You can pray for anything, and if you have faith, you will receive it." "

Judges 16:28 (NIV), "Then Samson prayed to the LORD, "Sovereign LORD, remember me. Please, God, strengthen me just once more, and let me with one blow get revenge on the Philistines for my two eyes."

1 Kings 8:26 (NKJV), "And now I pray, O God of Israel, let Your word come true, which You have spoken to Your servant David my father."

1 Kings 17:21 (GNT), "Then he prayed aloud, "O Lord my God, why have you done such a terrible thing to this widow? She has been kind enough to take care of me, and now you kill her son!" Then Elijah stretched himself out on the boy three times and prayed, "O Lord my God, restore this child to life!" The Lord answered Elijah's prayer; the child started breathing again and revived. Elijah took the boy back downstairs to his mother and said to her, "Look, your son is alive!" She answered, "Now I know that you are a man of God and that the Lord really speaks through you!""

1 Timothy 2:8 (NLT), "In every place of worship, I want men to pray with holy hands lifted up to God, free from anger and controversy."

James 1:5-8 (ESV), "Now if any of you lacks wisdom, he should ask God, who gives to everyone generously without a rebuke, and it will be given to him. But he must ask in faith, without any doubts, for the one who has doubts is like a wave of the sea that is driven and tossed by the wind. Such a person should not expect to receive anything from the Lord. He is a double-minded man, unstable in all he undertakes."

James 5:15 (GNT), "This prayer made in faith will heal the sick; the Lord will restore them to health, and the sins they have committed will be forgiven."

Mark 9:23 (NLT), ""What do you mean, 'If I can'?" Jesus asked. "Anything is possible if a person believes."

Luke 17:11-19, "While He was on the way to Jerusalem, He was passing between Samaria and Galilee. As He entered a village, ten leprous men who stood at a distance met Him; and they raised their voices, saying, "Jesus, Master, have mercy on us!" When He saw them, He said to them, "Go and show yourselves to the priests." And as they were going, they were cleansed. Now one of them, when he saw that he had been healed, turned back, glorifying God with a loud voice, and he fell on his face at His feet, giving thanks to Him. And he was a Samaritan. Then Jesus answered and said, "Were there not ten cleansed? But the nine—where are they? "Was no one found who returned to give glory to God, except this foreigner?" And He said to him, "Stand up and go; your faith has made you well.","

James 5:17 (ESV), "Elijah was a man with a nature like ours, and he prayed fervently that it might not rain, and for three years and six months it did not rain on the earth."

Galatians 3:1-9 (NKJV), "O foolish Galatians! Who has bewitched you that you should not obey the truth, before whose eyes Jesus Christ was clearly portrayed among you as crucified? This only I want to learn from you: Did you receive the Spirit by the works of the law, or by the hearing of faith? Are you so foolish? Having begun in the Spirit, are you now being made perfect by the flesh? Have you suffered so many things in vain—if indeed it was in vain? Therefore He who supplies the Spirit to you and works miracles among you, does He do it by the works of the law, or by the hearing of faith?— just as Abraham "believed God, and it was accounted to him for righteousness." Therefore know that only those who are of faith are sons of Abraham. And the Scripture, foreseeing that God would justify the Gentiles by faith, preached the gospel to Abraham beforehand, saying, "In you all the nations shall be blessed." So then those who are of faith are blessed with believing Abraham."

Hebrews 11:4 (CEV), "Because Abel had faith, he offered God a better sacrifice than Cain did. God was pleased with him and his gift, and even though Abel is now dead, his faith still speaks for him."

God responds to our faith. Our faith in God moves us to trust Him, to carry out his instructions, to work in believing, to act because you believe. Faith produces its fruit, and good works (Genesis 4:3-7; Hebrews 11:6; Isaiah 53: James 2:15-17). It's not trusting just in one's own work but a work that is a product of faith.

Chapter Five

IN CHRIST'S AUTHORITY

- In the name of Jesus Christ of Nazareth prayers are answered. His authority is undeniable to the Father in heaven. When we pray in His name, Jesus Christ of Nazareth, we are saying to God we have come in Christ's stead, because we realise you have highly exalted that name above all other names. That is powerful, because the believer is making a statement that in one's self there is nothing worthy to merit God's grace but that through Christ's atonement and sacrifice our prayers are heard, and we escape God's wrath or Him turning away. So, you ask in Christ's name.

- When we speak to Christ about our petitions, He brings it to God on our behalf, making intercessions for us. He says to us we can approach the Father God in His name and receive our petitions as granted. This is because we have a place of sonship, as a joint heirship with Christ. God hears us as He would His Son. It is as if a signet ring is on our hands who trust Christ when we approach the throne room. Also be in remembrance that Christ has authority to grant our request because the Father has placed all things in His hands, and because He is one with the God-head.

The person of God has never changed, though the revelation of His person and name has been progressive through the generations, and each true and constant as we grow in knowledge of Him. Christ is our King and Lord, great sacrifice and intercessor. If a generation needs deliverance from oppression, God would reveal Himself as deliverer, to those trusting Him for help in famine or in need you will see He is your sustainer and provider, to the one in need of healing as your healer, to a world in need of redemption and salvation from sin, the Lord is your salvation and perfect sacrifice for all- yes, different manifestations, yet the same God. Christ is manifested to save all who believe in Him.

This scripture reminds us to seek the will of God and knowledge about the power in the name of Christ, not many know of this. If you do not know of your inheritance in Christ and the blessing of invoking the blessings in the name of the Lord, how can your prayers be answered except by His mercies? – consider, Colossians 1:9 (NKJV), "For this reason we also, since the day we heard it, do not cease to pray for you, and to ask that you may be filled with the knowledge of His will in all wisdom and spiritual understanding"

1 Kings 18:21-24 (NASB), "Elijah came near to all the people and said, "How long will you hesitate between two opinions? If the LORD is God, follow Him; but if Baal, follow him." But the people did not answer him a word. Then Elijah said to the people, "I alone am left a prophet of the LORD, but Baal's prophets are 450 men. "Now let them give us two oxen; and let them choose one ox for themselves and cut it up, and place it on the wood, but put no fire under it; and I will prepare the other ox and lay it on the wood, and I will not put a fire under it. "Then you call on the name of your god, and I will call on the name of the LORD, and the God who answers by fire, He is God." And all the people said, "That is a good idea.""

Proverbs 18:10 (ISV), "The name of the LORD is a strong tower; a righteous person rushes to it and is lifted up above the danger."

Psalm 20:7 (NASB), "Some boast in chariots and some in horses, But we will boast in the name of the LORD, our God."

Matthew 6:9 (ISV), "Therefore, this is how you should pray: 'Our Father in heaven, may your name be kept holy."

Acts 4:12 (CEV), "Only Jesus has the power to save! His name is the only one in all the world that can save anyone."

Understanding the Lordship of Christ, and His call to personal relationship with God is a good place to begin.

John 14:12-14 (GNT), "I am telling you the truth: those who believe in me will do what I do—yes, they will do even greater things, because I am going to the Father. And I will do whatever you ask for in my name, so that the Father's glory will be shown through the Son. If you ask me for anything in my name, I will do it."

Matthew 7:21 (NIV), "'"Not everyone who says to me, 'Lord, Lord,' will enter the kingdom of heaven, but only the one who does the will of my Father who is in heaven."

1 John 2:22-23 (ESV), "Who is the liar but he who denies that Jesus is the Christ? This is the antichrist, he who denies the Father and the Son. No one who denies the Son has the Father. Whoever confesses the Son has the Father also."

Luke 6:46 (NLT), "So why do you keep calling me 'Lord, Lord!' when you don't do what I say?"

Isaiah 9:6 (ESV), "For to us a child is born, to us a son is given; and the government shall be upon his shoulder, and his name shall be called Wonderful Counselor, Mighty God, Everlasting Father, Prince of Peace."

Colossians 2:9 (NIV), "For in Christ all the fullness of the Deity lives in bodily form"

Mighty acts are wroth in the name of Jesus Christ. At the mention of His name in prayer God is seen glorified before many. This makes the Christian faith unique that God had exalted the name of Christ, that demons and their works are cast out. It is confidence in God and in His name that dispels darkness. To intercede in His authority. To stand and declare the counsel of heaven, in the name above all names. Consider these cases-

Acts 3:1-10 (NIV), "One day Peter and John were going up to the temple at the time of prayer—at three in the afternoon. Now a man who was lame from birth was being carried to the temple gate called Beautiful, where he was put every day to beg from those going into the temple courts. When he saw Peter and John about to enter, he asked them for money. Peter looked straight at him, as did John. Then Peter said, "Look at us!" So the man gave them his attention, expecting to get something from them. Then Peter said, "Silver or gold I do not have, but what I do have I give you. In the name of Jesus Christ of Nazareth, walk." Taking him by the right hand, he helped him up, and instantly the man's feet and ankles became strong. He jumped to his feet and began to walk. Then he went with them into the temple courts, walking and jumping, and praising God. When all the people saw him walking and praising God, they recognized him as the same man who used to sit begging at the temple gate called Beautiful, and they were filled with wonder and amazement at what had happened to him."

Acts 19:11-20 (NIV), "God did extraordinary miracles through Paul, so that even handkerchiefs and aprons that had touched him were taken to the sick, and their illnesses were cured and the evil spirits left them. Some Jews who went around driving out evil spirits tried to invoke the name of the Lord Jesus over those who were demon-possessed. They would say, "In the name of the Jesus whom Paul preaches, I command you to come out." Seven sons of Sceva, a Jewish chief priest, were doing this. One day the evil spirit answered them, "Jesus I know, and Paul I know about, but who are you?" Then the man who had the evil spirit jumped on them and overpowered them all. He gave them such a beating that they ran out of the house naked and bleeding. When this became known to the Jews and

Greeks living in Ephesus, they were all seized with fear, and the name of the Lord Jesus was held in high honor. Many of those who believed now came and openly confessed what they had done. A number who had practiced sorcery brought their scrolls together and burned them publicly. When they calculated the value of the scrolls, the total came to fifty thousand drachmas. In this way the word of the Lord spread widely and grew in power."

In Mark 16:17-18 (ESV), it says "And these signs will accompany those who believe: in my name they will cast out demons; they will speak in new tongues; they will pick up serpents with their hands; and if they drink any deadly poison, it will not hurt them; they will lay their hands on the sick, and they will recover.'"

What matters is the name of the Lord, not our human authority or names or lineage. The power that can stop the schemes of hell flow from heaven. Human names may open some doors from its influence, but the name of Jehovah is above all. Amen. We are carnal if we keep referencing ourselves and camp and forget about the author of the work.

1 Corinthians 3:4-7 (ERV), "For when one saith, I am of Paul; and another, I am of Apollos; are ye not men? What then is Apollos? and what is Paul? Ministers through whom ye believed; and each as the Lord gave to him. I planted, Apollos watered; but God gave the increase. So then neither is he that planteth anything, neither he that watereth; but God that giveth the increase."

Philippians 2:8-11 (GNT), "He was humble and walked the path of obedience all the way to death— his death on the cross. For this reason God raised him to the highest place above and gave him the name that is greater than any other name. And so, in honor of the name of Jesus all beings in heaven, on earth, and in the world below will fall on their knees, and all will openly proclaim that Jesus Christ is Lord, to the glory of God the Father."

Ephesians 3:14-21 (NKJV), "For this reason I bow my knees to the Father of our Lord Jesus Christ, from whom the whole family in heaven and earth is named, that He would grant you, according to the riches of His glory, to be strengthened with might through His Spirit in the inner man, that Christ may dwell in your hearts through faith; that you, being rooted and grounded in love, may be able to comprehend with all the saints what is the width and length and depth and height— to know the love of Christ which passes knowledge; that you may be filled with all the fullness of God. Now to Him who is able to do exceedingly abundantly above all that we ask or think, according to the power that works in us, to Him be glory in the church by Christ Jesus to all generations, forever and ever. Amen."

Revelations 19:11 (ISV), "Then I saw heaven standing open, and there was a white horse! Its rider is named Faithful and True. He administers justice and wages war righteously."

Romans 10:13 (CSB), "since there is no distinction between Jew and Greek, because the same Lord of all richly blesses all who call on him. For everyone who calls on the name of the Lord will be saved."

1 Corinthians 1:2 (NLT), "I am writing to God's church in Corinth, to you who have been called by God to be his own holy people. He made you holy by means of Christ Jesus, just as he did for all people everywhere who call on the name of our Lord Jesus Christ, their Lord and ours."

Psalm 116:3-4 (NLT), "Death wrapped its ropes around me; the terrors of the grave overtook me. I saw only trouble and sorrow. Then I called on the name of the LORD:

"Please, LORD, save me!""

Chapter Six

THE PRAYER OF FIVE MEN AND FIVE WOMEN IN THE SCRIPTURES

- In a selected case study from biblical scripture of five men and five women, we see a resolution towards prayer. I find their prayers in scriptures inspiring.

- These examples show us that prayer as preserved in scriptures share a substantial gender balance. Men were not weak to depend on God, women where not shy to cry out to God for help, both recognised ultimately God was in control. They each yearned for the move of God, for His intervention in their time. Each prayed in their unique way, seeking heaven's will on earth. As Jesus said to pray, recognising God's name is holy as we call on Him, and to say His will, desire, purpose be done on earth as it is in heaven. Then for each to ask for their needs to be met.

- So, what is your peculiar story? You can bring your need to God.

The prayer of Solomon, Jabez, Paul, Jesus Christ, and Bartimaeus

Bartimaeus, Mark 10:46-47 (NIV)

"When he heard that it was Jesus of Nazareth, he began to shout, "Jesus, Son of David, have mercy on me!" Many rebuked him and told him to be quiet, but he shouted all the more, "Son of David, have mercy on me! Jesus stopped and said, "Call him."

So they called to the blind man, "Cheer up! On your feet! He's calling you." Throwing his cloak aside, he jumped to his feet and came to Jesus.

"What do you want me to do for you?" Jesus asked him.

The blind man said, "Rabbi, I want to see."

"Go," said Jesus, "your faith has healed you." Immediately he received his sight and followed Jesus along the road."

Solomon, 1 Kings 8:54-61 (NIV)

"When Solomon had finished all these prayers and supplications to the Lord, he rose from before the altar of the Lord, where he had been kneeling with his hands spread out toward heaven. He stood and blessed the whole assembly of Israel in a loud voice, saying:

"Praise be to the Lord, who has given rest to his people Israel just as he promised. Not one word has failed of all the good promises he gave through his servant Moses. May the Lord our God be with us as he was with our ancestors; may he never leave us nor forsake us. May he turn our hearts to him, to walk in obedience to him and keep the commands, decrees and laws he gave our ancestors. And may these words of mine, which I have prayed before the Lord, be near to the Lord our God day and night, that he may uphold the cause of his servant and the cause of his people Israel according to each day's need, so that all the peoples of the earth may know that the Lord is God and that there is no other. And may your hearts be fully committed to the Lord our God, to live by his decrees and obey his commands, as at this time.""

The Lord Jesus Christ, John 17:21-22 (NLT),

"I am praying not only for these disciples but also for all who will ever believe in me through their message. I pray that they will all be one, just as you and I are one—as you are in me, Father, and I am in you. And may they be in us so that the world will believe you sent me."

Jabez, 1 Chronicles 4:10 (NASB)

"Now Jabez called on the God of Israel, saying, "Oh that You would bless me indeed and enlarge my border, and that Your hand might be with me, and that You would keep me from harm that it may not pain me!" And God granted him what he requested."

Paul, Ephesians 1:15-23 (GNB)

"For this reason, ever since I heard about your faith in the Lord Jesus and your love for all God's people, I have not stopped giving thanks for you, remembering you in my prayers. I keep asking that the God of our Lord Jesus Christ, the glorious Father, may give you the Spirit of wisdom and revelation, so that you may know him better. I pray that the eyes of your heart may be enlightened in order that you may know the hope to which he has called you, the riches of his glorious inheritance in his holy people, and his incomparably great power for us who believe. That power is the same as the mighty strength he exerted when he raised Christ from the dead and seated him at his right hand in the heavenly realms, far above all rule and authority, power and dominion, and every name that is invoked, not only in the present age but also in the one to come. And God placed all things under his feet and appointed him to be head over everything for the church, which is his body, the fullness of him who fills everything in every way."

The prayer of Mary, Martha, Hannah, Deborah and Miriam

Mary, Luke 1:38 (AMP)

"Then Mary said, "Behold, I am the servant of the Lord; may it be done to me according to your word." And the angel left her."

Martha and sister, John 11:2-7 (NASB)

"It was the Mary who anointed the Lord with ointment, and wiped His feet with her hair, whose brother Lazarus was sick. So the sisters sent word to Him, saying, "Lord, behold, he whom You love is sick." But when Jesus heard this, He said, "This sickness is not to end in death, but for the glory of God, so that the Son of God may be glorified by it." Now Jesus loved Martha and her sister and Lazarus. So when He heard that he was sick, He then stayed two days longer in the place where He was. Then after this He said to the disciples, "Let us go to Judea again.""

Hannah, 1 Samuel 1: 10-17 (NLT)

"Hannah was in deep anguish, crying bitterly as she prayed to the Lord. And she made this vow: "O Lord of Heaven's Armies, if you will look upon my sorrow and answer my prayer and give me a son, then I will give him back to you. He will be yours for his entire lifetime, and as a sign that he has been dedicated to the Lord, his hair will never be cut."

As she was praying to the Lord, Eli watched her. Seeing her lips moving but hearing no sound, he thought she had been drinking. "Must you come here drunk?" he demanded. "Throw away your wine!"

"Oh no, sir!" she replied. "I haven't been drinking wine or anything stronger. But I am very discouraged, and I was pouring out my heart to the Lord. Don't think I am a wicked woman! For I have been praying out of great anguish and sorrow."

"In that case," Eli said, "go in peace! May the God of Israel grant the request you have asked of him."

Deborah, Judges 5:31 (NIV)

"So may all your enemies perish, Lord!

But may all who love you be like the sun when it rises in its strength."

Miriam, Exodus 15:11-13 (NIV)

"Who among the gods is like you, Lord?

Who is like you— majestic in holiness, awesome in glory, working wonders?

"You stretch out your right hand, and the earth swallows your enemies.

In your unfailing love you will lead the people you have redeemed.

In your strength you will guide them to your holy dwelling."

Chapter Seven

PRAYER OF THE PERSECUTED CHURCH

- The persecuted need us to support them in relief but more importantly to pray with them in their distress.

- God hears and releases strength and deliverance supernaturally. The scripture tells us of the comfort many found and the deliverances some experienced in their days.

Christ leaves us an admonishing of how to respond to persecution- pray. Consider:

Matthew 5:9-12 (ISV), "How blessed are those who make peace, because it is they who will be called God's children! "How blessed are those who are persecuted for righteousness' sake, because the kingdom from heaven belongs to them! "How blessed are you whenever people insult you, persecute you, and say all sorts of evil things against you falsely because of me! Rejoice and be extremely glad, because your reward in heaven is great! That's how they persecuted the prophets who came before you."

Matthew 5:43-48 (ISV), "You have heard that it was said, 'You must love your neighbor' and hate your enemy. But I say to you, love your enemies, and pray for those who persecute you, so that you will become children of your Father in heaven, because he makes his sun rise on both evil and good people, and he lets rain fall on the righteous and the unrighteous. If you love those who love you, what reward will you have? Even the tax collectors do the same, don't they? And if you greet only your relatives, that's no great thing you're doing, is it? Even the unbelievers do the same, don't they? So be perfect, as your heavenly Father is perfect."

Matthew 24:20 (NKJV), "And pray that your flight may not be in winter or on the Sabbath. For then there will be great tribulation, such as has not been since the beginning of the world until this time, no, nor ever shall be. And unless those days were shortened, no flesh would be saved; but for the elect's sake those days will be shortened."

Luke 21:36 (NIV), "Be always on the watch, and pray that you may be able to escape all that is about to happen, and that you may be able to stand before the Son of Man."

Luke 22:39-46 (GNT), "Jesus left the city and went, as he usually did, to the Mount of Olives; and the disciples went with him. When he arrived at the place, he said to them, "Pray that you will not fall into temptation." Then he went off from them about the distance of a stone's throw and knelt down and prayed. "Father," he said, "if you will, take this cup of suffering away from me. Not my will, however, but your will be done." An angel from heaven appeared to him and strengthened him. In great anguish he prayed even more fervently; his sweat was like drops of blood falling to the ground. Rising from his prayer, he went back to the disciples and found them asleep, worn out by their grief. He said to them, "Why are you sleeping? Get up and pray that you will not fall into temptation.""

John 17:15 (ESV), "I do not ask that you take them out of the world, but that you keep them from the evil one."

This was what Stephen did in the face of persecution:

Acts 7:59-60 (NLT), "As they stoned him, Stephen prayed, "Lord Jesus, receive my spirit." He fell to his knees, shouting, "Lord, don't charge them with this sin!" And with that, he died."

Also, in Exodus 3:7-10 (NLT), "Then the LORD told him, "I have certainly seen the oppression of my people in Egypt. I have heard their cries of distress because of their harsh slave drivers. Yes, I am aware of their suffering. So I have come down to rescue them from the power of the Egyptians and lead them out of Egypt into their own fertile and spacious land. It is a land flowing with milk and honey—the land where the Canaanites, Hittites, Amorites, Perizzites, Hivites, and Jebusites now live. Look! The cry of the people of Israel has reached me, and I have seen how harshly the Egyptians abuse them. Now go, for I am sending you to Pharaoh. You must lead my people Israel out of Egypt.""

How about God's deliverance of those young men who placed their confidence in God when the practice of their faith was put to the test, in Daniel 3:16-18 (NIV)- "Shadrach, Meshach and Abednego replied to him, "King Nebuchadnezzar, we do not need to defend ourselves before you in this matter. If we are thrown into the blazing furnace, the God we serve is able to deliver us from it, and he will deliver us from Your Majesty's hand. But even if he does not, we want you to know, Your Majesty, that we will not serve your gods or worship the image of gold you have set up."

Daniel 3: 25-30 (NIV) "He said, "Look! I see four men walking around in the fire, unbound and unharmed, and the fourth looks like a son of the gods." Nebuchadnezzar then approached the opening of the blazing furnace and shouted, "Shadrach, Meshach and Abednego, servants of the Most High God, come out! Come here!" So Shadrach, Meshach and Abednego came out of the fire, and the satraps, prefects, governors and royal advisers crowded around them. They saw that the fire had not harmed their bodies, nor was a hair of their heads singed; their robes were not scorched, and there was no smell of fire on them. Then Nebuchadnezzar said, "Praise be to the God of Shadrach, Meshach and Abednego, who has sent his angel and rescued his servants! They trusted in him and defied the king's command and were willing to give up their lives rather than serve or worship any god except their own God. Therefore I decree that the people of any nation or language who say anything against the God of Shadrach, Meshach and Abednego be cut into pieces and their houses be turned into piles of rubble, for no other god can save in this way." Then the king promoted Shadrach, Meshach and Abednego in the province of Babylon."

A prayer (especially as a Church praying for heaven's intervention, I found it potent).

For the persecuted Church to continually triumph over the gates of hell.

For the peace of God to continually rest over His people in every nation, and the gospel to advance effectively.

For God to distinguish His true servants and shepherds- those who care for the flock, from hirelings, so the body of Christ will be strengthened as they mark those who pleasure in division and avoid them.

For those 'legally empowered' to act in defence of lives and properties to do so effectively, especially Christians and every other vulnerable persons (people) in hostile places- to ability to tell what difference, and specific approach needed, for lasting peace.

For wisdom to be thankful, as we weigh our burdens in relation to that which others bear, and to see the grace and purpose of God beyond our righteousness.

For oneness in the body, as Christ is one with the Father continually, so the Church might be formidable in showcasing the love of God.

For grace to continue in prayers and worship to keep seeing your hand of deliverance(s). And for wisdom for those who serve as leaders, to remember your sovereignty.

In the name of Jesus Christ. [John 10:1-18; Romans 16:17; Galatians 6:2; Matthew 16 :18, 5:44; 1 Timothy 2:2]

Chapter Eight

PRAYER FOR SPIRITUAL FIRE (REVIVAL)

- This is a prayer for grace to operate in your spiritual calling, office and assignment.

- Spiritual fire speaks of fervency, also potency, which burns up debris that restricts or seeks to impede your movement towards your God-given goal.

Bless God that Christ would not thrust His disciples into work without first equipping them. He said first, wait. Second, whilst waiting, pray. Wait in prayer, and what were they to pray about? – spiritual fervency, the grace for urgency which God supplies. This comes by the presence of God's Spirit. The Holy Spirit when He come would do this. He would grant even the grace to pray more and the wisdom to pray right. It's a cue to a more deeper and refreshing experience.

Here we see Christ's instruction- Luke 24:49 (NLT), "You are witnesses of all these things. "And now I will send the Holy Spirit, just as my Father promised. But stay here in the city until the Holy Spirit comes and fills you with power from heaven." Then Jesus led them to Bethany, and lifting his hands to heaven, he blessed them."

In Acts 2:2-4 (GNT), we see what happened as they obeyed-

"Suddenly there was a noise from the sky which sounded like a strong wind blowing, and it filled the whole house where they were sitting. Then they saw what looked like tongues of fire which spread out and touched each person there. They were all filled with the Holy Spirit and began to talk in other languages, as the Spirit enabled them to speak."

God began to bear the Apostles witness thereafter, their prayers were answered as God poured His Spirit as they ministered, on believers-

Acts 8:17 (CEV), "Peter and John then placed their hands on everyone who had faith in the Lord, and they were given the Holy Spirit."

The call to pray is a divine one, a necessity, borne out of the fervency of the Spirit. I perceive as we step out in faith the Spirit of God catches up with us and takes over. It is as if He watches to see if you are hungry and then 'woosh' there is a surge of water that comes and fills the thirsty and covers the dry ground. Consider these Scriptures:

Jude 1:20-21 (NASB), "But you, beloved, building yourselves up on your most holy faith, praying in the Holy Spirit, keep yourselves in the love of God, waiting anxiously for the mercy of our Lord Jesus Christ to eternal life."

Matthew 17:18-21 (NKJV), "And Jesus rebuked the demon, and it came out of him; and the child was cured from that very hour. Then the disciples came to Jesus privately and said, "Why could we not cast it out?" So Jesus said to them, "Because of your unbelief; for assuredly, I say to you, if you have faith as a mustard seed, you will say to this mountain, 'Move from here to there,' and it will move; and nothing will be impossible for you. However, this kind does not go out except by prayer and fasting."

Romans 12:11-12 (NLT), "Never be lazy, but work hard and serve the Lord enthusiastically. Rejoice in our confident hope. Be patient in trouble, and keep on praying."

Ephesians 6:10-20 (ERV), "Finally, be strong in the Lord, and in the strength of his might. Put on the whole armour of God, that ye may be able to stand against the wiles of the devil. For our wrestling is not against flesh and blood, but against the principalities, against the powers, against the world-rulers of this darkness, against the spiritual hosts of wickedness in the heavenly places. Wherefore take up the whole armour of God, that ye may be able to withstand in the evil day, and, having done all, to stand. Stand therefore, having girded your loins with truth, and having put on the breastplate of righteousness, and having shod your feet with the preparation of the gospel of peace; withal taking up the shield of faith, wherewith ye shall be able to quench all the fiery darts of the evil one. And take the helmet of salvation, and the sword of the Spirit, which is the word of God: with all prayer and supplication praying at all seasons in the Spirit, and watching thereunto in all perseverance and supplication for all the saints"

1 Thessalonians 5:16-19 (NLT), "Always be joyful. Never stop praying. Be thankful in all circumstances, for this is God's will for you who belong to Christ Jesus. Do not stifle the Holy Spirit."

Luke 19:45-46 (NIV), "When Jesus entered the temple courts, he began to drive out those who were selling. "It is written," he said to them, " 'My house will be a house of prayer'; but you have made it 'a den of robbers.'"

Luke 18:1-8 (NKJV), "Then He spoke a parable to them, that men always ought to pray and not lose heart, saying: "There was in a certain city a judge who did not fear God nor regard man. Now there was a widow in that city; and she came to him, saying, 'Get justice for me from my adversary.' And he would not for a while; but afterward he said within himself, 'Though I do not fear God nor regard man, yet because this widow troubles me I will avenge her, lest by her continual coming she weary me.' "Then the Lord said, "Hear what the unjust judge said. And shall God not avenge His own elect who cry out day and night to Him, though He bears long with them? I tell you that He will avenge them speedily. Nevertheless, when the Son of Man comes, will He really find faith on the earth?"

WATCH ONE HOUR? – 'OUGHT-NESS' OF PRAYER

- Why watch or pray for "one hour"? I suppose it points to Christ's emphasis on perseverance in spiritual conversation with God.

- It could also mean more or less of the hour, it is more a pointer and symbolism to a staying ability with God until you perceive your petition is heard. Slumbering when you ought to tarry means you have given up on God's ability to listen.

- There is also a level of grace, where it's not a question of just time but being lost in His presence, that you stay awake enjoying fellowship. This is a call to less apathy, but more a desire to fellowship.

- Christ is the epitome of deep reverence for God- a gladness of heart to enjoy the presence of God, a sincerity shown in openness towards God, a belief that the exercise of prayer do really make a difference spiritually, that spirituality with Jehovah could bring earthly results. Christ leads by example. I think He understands our limitations and urges us on to push, to shake off the slumbering and pray a little more, showing in God our dependence on Him. We truly ought to pray, and pray like Jesus did, not only in His words as in Matthew 6:9-13 but also in His style of perseverance- in some cases an hour, other cases praying all night, some other times a trek to the mountains, other times seeking a secret place, also considering the temple of God as a place of prayer, and also using other places of quiet to pray- even the garden of Gethsemane. It seems to me, that to the Lord prayer constituted His formidable makeup.

- Prayer demonstrates your personal relationship with God and creates an opportunity for depth of conversation- an opportunity to express your thoughts heavenward, and then at the timing of God to wait for His response. At this present time and place, it is not about others' relationship with God but yours. In all the buzz, that hush, that waiting before a monumental decision, that discipline to commend to the sovereign God your affairs before setting out, has never been so needed. All the energy could so easily be burnt out with you back to square one without God, perhaps it's this clarity of insight that brings us back to our knees, saying "God, so what would you have me do this time?"

Let us consider Jesus' life and teaching to His disciples, in-

Luke 6:12 (ESV), "In these days he went out to the mountain to pray, and all night he continued in prayer to God. And when day came, he called his disciples and chose from them twelve, whom he named apostles: Simon, whom he named Peter, and Andrew his brother, and James and John, and Philip, and Bartholomew, and Matthew, and Thomas, and James the son of Alphaeus, and Simon who was called the Zealot, and Judas the son of James, and Judas Iscariot, who became a traitor."

Luke 22:45 (NLT), "At last he stood up again and returned to the disciples, only to find them asleep, exhausted from grief. "Why are you sleeping?" he asked them. "Get up and pray, so that you will not give in to temptation.""

Luke 18:1 (ESV), "And he told them a parable to the effect that they ought always to pray and not lose heart."

James 5:16 (NASB), "Therefore, confess your sins to one another, and pray for one another so that you may be healed. The effective prayer of a righteous man can accomplish much."

Matthew 17:1-9 (GWT), "After six days Jesus took Peter, James, and John (the brother of James) and led them up a high mountain where they could be alone. Jesus' appearance changed in front of them. His face became as bright as the sun and his clothes as white as light. Suddenly, Moses and Elijah appeared to them and were talking with Jesus. Peter said to Jesus, "Lord, it's good that we're here. If you want, I'll put up three tents here- one for you, one for Moses, and one for Elijah." He was still speaking when a bright cloud overshadowed them. Then a voice came out of the cloud and said, "This is my Son, whom I love and with whom I am pleased. Listen to him!" The disciples were terrified when they heard this and fell facedown on the ground. But Jesus touched them and said, "Get up, and don't be afraid!" As they raised their heads, they saw no one but Jesus. On their way down the mountain, Jesus ordered them, "Don't tell anyone what you have seen. Wait until the Son of Man has been brought back to life."

Moses similarly has an incredible attitude of also spending time with the Lord, and it affected his relations with others. They left him for a while, his brightness was from heaven.

Exodus 34:28-35 (NLT), "Moses remained there on the mountain with the LORD forty days and forty nights. In all that time he ate no bread and drank no water. And the LORD wrote the terms of the covenant—the Ten Commandments—on the stone tablets. When Moses came down Mount Sinai carrying the two stone tablets inscribed with the terms of the covenant, he wasn't aware that his face had become radiant because he had spoken to the LORD. So when Aaron and the people of Israel saw the radiance of Moses' face, they were afraid to come near him. But Moses called out to them and asked Aaron and all the leaders of the community to come over, and he talked with them. Then all the people of Israel approached him, and Moses gave them all the instructions the LORD had given him on Mount Sinai. When Moses finished speaking with them, he covered his face with a veil. But whenever he went into the Tent of Meeting to speak with the LORD, he would remove the veil until he came out again. Then he would give the people whatever instructions the LORD had given him, and the people of Israel would see the radiant glow of his face. So he would put the veil over his face until he returned to speak with the LORD."

Jesus encouraged His disciples and those who believed to wait for the outpour of the Spirit- see what happens.

Luke 24: 49 (GWT), "I'm sending you what my Father promised. Wait here in the city until you receive power from heaven."

Acts 2:1-17 (CEV), "On the day of Pentecost all the Lord's followers were together in one place. Suddenly there was a noise from heaven like the sound of a mighty wind! It filled the house where they were meeting. Then they saw what looked like fiery tongues moving in all directions, and a tongue came and settled on each person there. The Holy Spirit took control of everyone, and they began speaking whatever languages the Spirit let them speak. Many religious Jews from every country in the world were living in Jerusalem. And when they heard this noise, a crowd gathered. But they were surprised, because they were hearing everything in their own languages. They were excited and amazed, and said: Don't all these who are speaking come from Galilee? Then why do we hear them speaking our very own languages? Some of us are from Parthia, Media, and Elam. Others are from Mesopotamia, Judea, Cappadocia, Pontus, Asia, Phrygia, Pamphylia, Egypt, parts of Libya near Cyrene, Rome, Crete, and Arabia. Some of us were born Jews, and others of us have chosen to be Jews. Yet we all hear them using our own languages to tell the wonderful things God has done. Everyone was excited and confused. Some of them even kept asking each other, "What does all this mean?" Others made fun of the Lord's followers and said, "They are drunk." Peter stood with the eleven apostles and spoke in a loud and clear voice to the crowd: Friends and everyone else living in Jerusalem, listen carefully to what I have to say! You are wrong to think that these people are drunk. After all, it is only nine o'clock in the morning. But this is what God told the prophet Joel to say, "When the last days come, I will give my Spirit to everyone. Your sons and daughters will prophesy. Your young men will see visions, and your old men will have dreams."

Prophet Isaiah prophesied, that as God's people shook off complacency and waited on God the coming of His Spirit would bring in life and healing.

Isaiah 32:11-17 (NLT), "Tremble, you women of ease; throw off your complacency. Strip off your pretty clothes, and put on burlap to show your grief. Beat your breasts in sorrow for your bountiful farms and your fruitful grapevines. For your land will be overgrown with thorns and briers. Your joyful homes and happy towns will be gone. The palace and the city will be deserted, and busy towns will be empty. Wild donkeys will frolic and flocks will graze in the empty forts and watchtowers until at last the Spirit is poured out on us from heaven. Then the wilderness will become a fertile field, and the fertile field will yield bountiful crops. Justice will rule in the wilderness and righteousness in the fertile field. And this righteousness will bring peace. Yes, it will bring quietness and confidence forever."

Isaiah 62:6-7 (GWT), "I have posted watchmen on your walls, Jerusalem. They will never be silent day or night. Whoever calls on the LORD, do not give yourselves any rest, and do not give him any rest until he establishes Jerusalem and makes it an object of praise throughout the earth."

Isaiah 40:29-31 (ESV), "He gives power to the faint, and to him who has no might he increases strength. Even youths shall faint and be weary, and young men shall fall exhausted; but they who wait for the LORD shall renew their strength; they shall mount up with wings like eagles; they shall run and not be weary; they shall walk and not faint."

Chapter Ten

WATCH AND PRAY

- By all means pray, but also in the Spirit observe the change of the spiritual wind, the change of sound for abundance, to know when victory is had.

- Also, avoid unbelief going forward. But persevere in prayer- this speaks more to an alertness to prayer not just the 'oughtness.' An awareness of the spiritual climate and being able to shift the gears forward in pressure and backwards in thanksgiving, knowing when you need to intensify and when to come back rejoicing. Elijah prayed the more, again and again, as he saw the cloud waiting for a sign, so when he saw the form of a hand supernaturally in the cloud, he knew God had heard him, so stood up. It is as if knocking the doors of heaven for a response.

- The questions are these, in prayer- Is there a warning? Is there an alarm? Is there a change of season, and movement in the Spirit?

These principles show us how to pray and how to also balance what is happening around you in response to prayer. No one wants to keep filling a full car tank, or similarly keep requesting for what has been answered in prayer. That harmony of balancing practical progress which is in response to prayer and knowing when to continue. It could also extend to managing expectations or being careful to not ignore what may be essential to your living.

Consider these Scriptures:

James 5:17-18 (NLT), "Elijah was as human as we are, and yet when he prayed earnestly that no rain would fall, none fell for three and a half years! Then, when he prayed again, the sky sent down rain and the earth began to yield its crops."

1 Kings 18: 42-44 (NLT), "So Ahab went to eat and drink. But Elijah climbed to the top of Mount Carmel and bowed low to the ground and prayed with his face between his knees. Then he said to his servant, "Go and look out toward the sea." The servant went and looked, then returned to Elijah and said, "I didn't see anything." Seven times Elijah told him to go and look. Finally the seventh time, his servant told him, "I saw a little cloud about the size of a man's hand rising from the sea." Then Elijah shouted, "Hurry to Ahab and tell him, 'Climb into your chariot and go back home. If you don't hurry, the rain will stop you!'"

Judges 6:36-40 (NLT), "Then Gideon said to God, "If you are truly going to use me to rescue Israel as you promised, prove it to me in this way. I will put a wool fleece on the threshing floor tonight. If the fleece is wet with dew in the morning but the ground is dry, then I will know that you are going to help me rescue Israel as you promised." And that is just what happened. When Gideon got up early the next morning, he squeezed the fleece and wrung out a whole bowlful of water. Then Gideon said to God, "Please don't be angry with me, but let me make one more request. Let me use the fleece for one more test. This time let the fleece remain dry while the ground around it is wet with dew." So that night God did as Gideon asked. The fleece was dry in the morning, but the ground was covered with dew."

As I earlier mentioned, prayer is communing with God in faith and listening for His response. Prayer could be in response to news which may have been favourable or not; and could also be on the basis of a collective decision to consecrate a period of time to prayer- not neglecting what could be practically useful. For example, you may need to pray, but when it is time take your children to their study or place of care. In whatever context you pray, but consider in relation to whether be family, work life, for grace to navigate persecution or temptation, health issues and so on. Christian prayer shows us it is not empty babblings, but in response to specific situations, so the need to also be watchful to monitor the situation until the hand of God for intervention is seen.

1 Corinthians 7:5 (CEV), "So don't refuse sex to each other, unless you agree not to have sex for a little while, in order to spend time in prayer. Then Satan won't be able to tempt you because of your lack of self-control."

2 Corinthians 1:8-11 (ESV)," For we do not want you to be unaware, brothers, of the affliction we experienced in Asia. For we were so utterly burdened beyond our strength that we despaired of life itself. Indeed, we felt that we had received the sentence of death. But that was to make us rely not on ourselves but on God who raises the dead. He delivered us from such a deadly peril, and he will deliver us. On him we have set our hope that he will deliver us again. You also must help us by prayer, so that many will give thanks on our behalf for the blessing granted us through the prayers of many."

Colossians 4:1-4 (ISR), "Masters, give your servants what is righteous and fair, knowing that you also have a Master in the heavens. Continue in prayer, watching therein, with thanksgiving, praying at the same time also for us, that Elohim would open to us a door for the word, to speak the secret of Messiah, for which I am also in chains, so that I make it clear, as I should speak."

1 Peter 4:7 (NKJV), "But the end of all things is at hand; therefore be serious and watchful in your prayers."

Matthew 26:41 (NASB), "Keep watching and praying that you may not enter into temptation; the spirit is willing, but the flesh is weak."

Mark 13:32-37 (CEV), "No one knows the day or the time. The angels in heaven don't know, and the Son himself doesn't know. Only the Father knows. So watch out and be ready! You don't know when the time will come. It is like what happens when a man goes away for a while and places his servants in charge of everything. He tells each of them what to do, and he orders the guard to keep alert. So be alert! You don't know when the master of the house will come back. It could be in the evening or at midnight or before dawn or in the morning. But if he comes suddenly, don't let him find you asleep. I tell everyone just what I have told you. Be alert!"

Chapter Eleven

MANNERS OF PRAYER

- There are several forms of prayer according to scriptures. A believer must recognise this and seek to delve into all forms of prayer.
- There is also an attitude to prayer, if you must see answers.

Isaiah 37:14-20 (NIV), "Hezekiah received the letter from the messengers and read it. Then he went up to the temple of the Lord and spread it out before the Lord. And Hezekiah prayed to the Lord: "Lord Almighty, the God of Israel, enthroned between the cherubim, you alone are God over all the kingdoms of the earth. You have made heaven and earth. Give ear, Lord, and hear; open your eyes, Lord, and see; listen to all the words Sennacherib has sent to ridicule the living God. "It is true, Lord, that the Assyrian kings have laid waste all these peoples and their lands. They have thrown their gods into the fire and destroyed them, for they were not gods but only wood and stone, fashioned by human hands. Now, Lord our

God, deliver us from his hand, so that all the kingdoms of the earth may know that you, Lord, are the only God."

Daniel 9:17 (NIV), "Now, our God, hear the prayers and petitions of your servant. For your sake, Lord, look with favor on your desolate sanctuary."

Acts 12:5 (NLT), "But while Peter was in prison, the church prayed very earnestly for him."

Romans 10:1 (NKJV), "Brethren, my heart's desire and prayer to God for Israel is that they may be saved."

Ephesians 6:18 (ISV), "Pray in the Spirit at all times with every kind of prayer and request. Likewise, be alert with your most diligent efforts and pray for all the saints."

Philippians 1:3-4 (NKJV), "I thank my God upon every remembrance of you, always in every prayer of mine making request for you all with joy"

Romans 1:8-12 (GNT), "First, I thank my God through Jesus Christ for all of you, because the whole world is hearing about your faith. God is my witness that what I say is true—the God whom I serve with all my heart by preaching the Good News about his Son. God knows that I remember you every time I pray. I ask that God in his good will may at last make it possible for me to visit you now. For I want very much to see you, in order to share a spiritual blessing with you to make you strong. What I mean is that both you and I will be helped at the same time, you by my faith and I by yours."

1 Timothy 2:1-4 (GNT), "First of all, then, I urge that petitions, prayers, requests, and thanksgivings be offered to God for all people; for kings and all others who are in authority, that we may live a quiet and peaceful life with all reverence toward God and with proper conduct. This is good and it pleases God our Savior, who wants everyone to be saved and to come to know the truth."

1 Corinthians 14:13-17 (NLT), "So anyone who speaks in tongues should pray also for the ability to interpret what has been said. For if I pray in tongues, my spirit is praying, but I don't understand what I am saying. Well then, what shall I do? I will pray in the spirit, and I will also pray in

words I understand. I will sing in the spirit, and I will also sing in words I understand. For if you praise God only in the spirit, how can those who don't understand you praise God along with you? How can they join you in giving thanks when they don't understand what you are saying? You will be giving thanks very well, but it won't strengthen the people who hear you."

John 17:9-10 (ESV), "I am praying for them. I am not praying for the world but for those whom you have given me, for they are yours. All mine are yours, and yours are mine, and I am glorified in them."

Numbers 23:11-12 (ESV), "And Balak said to Balaam, "What have you done to me? I took you to curse my enemies, and behold, you have done nothing but bless them." And he answered and said, "Must I not take care to speak what the LORD puts in my mouth?"

Jeremiah 29:7 (NASB), "Seek the welfare of the city where I have sent you into exile, and pray to the LORD on its behalf; for in its welfare you will have welfare."

Jeremiah 37:3 (NLT), "Nevertheless, King Zedekiah sent Jehucal son of Shelemiah, and Zephaniah the priest, son of Maaseiah, to ask Jeremiah, "Please pray to the LORD our God for us."

Ecclesiastics 5:1 (GNT), "Be careful about going to the Temple. It is better to go there to learn than to offer sacrifices like foolish people who don't know right from wrong."

Psalm 107:21-22 (NLT), "Let them praise the LORD for his great love and for the wonderful things he has done for them. Let them offer sacrifices of thanksgiving and sing joyfully about his glorious acts."

Isaiah 56:7 (GNT), "And the Lord says to those foreigners who become part of his people, who love him and serve him, who observe the Sabbath and faithfully keep his covenant: "I will bring you to Zion, my sacred hill, give you joy in my house of prayer, and accept the sacrifices you offer on my altar. My Temple will be called a house of prayer for the people of all nations." The Sovereign Lord, who has brought his people Israel home from exile, has promised that he will bring still other people to join them."

Chapter Twelve

RESPONSE TO ANSWERS IN APPRECIATION

- When God hears your prayers, you ought to be thankful.
- We can also bring an offering in appreciation.
- Be careful to maintain your testimony of God's goodness.
- Stay humble and encourage others to consider the move of God at work.
- Refer others to the source, which is Christ.

Job 22:26-28 (NLT), "Then you will take delight in the Almighty and look up to God. You will pray to him, and he will hear you, and you will fulfil your vows to him. You will succeed in whatever you choose to do, and light will shine on the road ahead of you."

Luke 17:11 19 (CEV), "On his way to Jerusalem, Jesus went along the border between Samaria and Galilee. As he was going into a village, ten men with leprosy came toward him. They stood at a distance and shouted, "Jesus, Master, have pity on us!" Jesus looked at them and said, "Go show yourselves to the priests." On their way they were healed. When one of them discovered that he was healed, he came back, shouting praises to

God. He bowed down at the feet of Jesus and thanked him. The man was from the country of Samaria. Jesus asked, "Weren't ten men healed? Where are the other nine? Why was this foreigner the only one who came back to thank God?" Then Jesus told the man, "You may get up and go. Your faith has made you well."

Malachi 1:6-9 (GNT), "The Lord Almighty says to the priests, "Children honor their parents, and servants honor their masters. I am your father—why don't you honor me? I am your master—why don't you respect me? You despise me, and yet you ask, 'How have we despised you?' This is how—by offering worthless food on my altar. Then you ask, 'How have we failed to respect you?' I will tell you—by showing contempt for my altar. When you bring a blind or sick or lame animal to sacrifice to me, do you think there's nothing wrong with that? Try giving an animal like that to the governor! Would he be pleased with you or grant you any favors?" Now, you priests, try asking God to be good to us. He will not answer your prayer, and it will be your fault."

Ecclesiastics 5:4-6 (NASB), "When you make a vow to God, do not be late in paying it; for He takes no delight in fools. Pay what you vow! It is better that you should not vow than that you should vow and not pay. Do not let your speech cause you to sin and do not say in the presence of the messenger of God that it was a mistake. Why should God be angry on account of your voice and destroy the work of your hands?"

A vow is a promise you make to God in integrity and in demonstration of your faith, that if He answers your prayer you will fulfil. God then expects you keep it, because He measured your heart as willing, trusting, and deeply desiring His move, so to turn around and refuse to honour Him, mocks His graciousness. It is for example saying if God preserves you in a perilous journey you are about to undertake, or enables you to successfully complete an educational programme, you would come into the Church to pray before Him in thanksgiving, or tell your friends that God deserves credit, as the accomplishment was beyond your dexterity or wit. Or perhaps the promise you made in secret was to make a donation to support God's work, or give a gift to any of God's servant that supported you in that time or prayed with you, or maybe help a child through their orphanage or school, whatever the promise was- to do it brings God pleasure. Prayer can be more complex than just words, there is an exchange of terms, when God does His acts, do yours. Whatever we do for the Lord should be borne out of the place of love- consider Mary's attitude in John 12:3.

Below is an exposition, I was priviledged to teach and preach on, on invitation in a URC Church in Weoley Castle, Birmingham, sometime in 2019 on Luke 17:11-19- five biblical principles to consider on gratitude to God. I think you would find it also relevant and helpful to this section on appreciation.

Read further Colossians 3:15; Psalm 100:4

Luke 17: 11-19 can be contrasted with 2 Samuel 7:1-29. In the first one of the healed lepers returned with a cheerful and thankful heart and had God's approval, whilst the majority had a rebuke; on the other scripture we also see David express thanks remembering where God brought him from in his prayers, from the farm to the palace.

God would boast of Abraham and David- but see their heart. A heart of reverence. Genesis 18:17-19; 2 Samuel 7:18.

Five principles:

i. God expects gratitude in response to good news v.17

ii. God's love is not necessarily based on our pre-gratitude v.13-14

iii. There is more blessing for the thankful and divine affirmation v.19

iv. Be sure to stand alone than with the crowd if on right standing with God. Do not be obsessed on togetherness. v.15

v. You do well to obey but also consider a heart of thankfulness continually. v. 14; 1 Thessalonians 5:16

To be cleansed is to be healed, but to be whole comes from the Greek word *sozo* meaning to be protected, preserved, also healed and to do well. There is more a sense of completeness (and also, a sense that what they have received is preserved). Christ imparts a double blessing, twice he said be healed. Mark 8:22-26, also Christ blesses a man twice, so take notice when God intervenes in this manner- usually once will so. But God I think emphasises to demonstrate his Lordship and to bring wholeness. Psalm 62:11-12.

If the heart bear seeds of thanksgiving it would bear a fruit full of it. Psalm 126:6. Lets' remember whilst we come to God to give our gifts or offering in appreciation for what he has done for us, the heart is key, being profoundly grateful to recognise the goodness of God. Mark 12:43; Genesis 4:3-7

There will be opportunity to sing another's praise and help a friend, but gratitude to God is owing your well doing to God, for some that's painful because they think all they are have come from self-effort. Also, gratitude could be in expression of a gift or words that show appreciation, as we see in this case of the man who returned.

Chapter Thirteen

HUMILITY IN PRAYER, RIGHTEOUSNESS, THE PEACE OF GOD

- God resists the proud- so, a posture, language, heart of humility is necessary in prayer. Humility also means not claiming a right in sin, acknowledging that God takes no delight in iniquity, so you choose not to. But rather to desire His mercy and grace.

- The thought of God not listening is bewildering, though a person cries for help- the imagery is intense. But the question is why? It seems God can see behind some of those tears whether there is pride in sin, a willingness to hold a stake against God, and to not trust Him. The human mind may only judge the visible expressions and act, but God sees far much more. Such prayer does not trigger compassion from God but a rebuke. For God it must be like a drunk and proud misfit who has done wrong, before a glorious King insisting the ruler do His errands- it must be the arrogance that puts Him off. Humility before a great God requires a heart that is not lifted. This God who cannot be seen and dwells in the heavens sees the heart that loves Him.

Proverbs 15:8 (NIV), "The LORD detests the sacrifice of the wicked, but the prayer of the upright pleases him."

Verse 25, "The LORD tears down the house of the proud, but he sets the widow's boundary stones in place."

Proverbs 28:9 (NIV), "If anyone turns a deaf ear to my instruction, even their prayers are detestable."

Jeremiah 7:16-20 (NLT) "Pray no more for these people, Jeremiah. Do not weep or pray for them, and don't beg me to help them, for I will not listen to you. Don't you see what they are doing throughout the towns of Judah and in the streets of Jerusalem? No wonder I am so angry! Watch how the children gather wood and the fathers build sacrificial fires. See how the women knead dough and make cakes to offer to the Queen of Heaven. And they pour out liquid offerings to their other idol gods! Am I the one they are hurting?" asks the LORD. "Most of all, they hurt themselves, to their own shame." So this is what the Sovereign LORD says: "I will pour out my terrible fury on this place. Its people, animals, trees, and crops will be consumed by the unquenchable fire of my anger."

Jeremiah 11:14-17 (NIV), "Do not pray for this people or offer any plea or petition for them, because I will not listen when they call to me in the time of their distress. "What is my beloved doing in my temple as she, with many others, works out her evil schemes? Can consecrated meat avert your punishment? When you engage in your wickedness, then you rejoice." The Lord called you a thriving olive tree with fruit beautiful in form. But with the roar of a mighty storm he will set it on fire, and its branches will be broken. The Lord Almighty, who planted you, has decreed disaster for you, because the people of both Israel and Judah have done evil and aroused my anger by burning incense to Baal."

Isaiah 1:15-18 (GWT), "So when you stretch out your hands [in prayer], I will turn my eyes away from you. Even though you offer many prayers, I will not listen because your hands are covered with blood. "Wash yourselves! Become clean! Get your evil deeds out of my sight. Stop doing evil. Learn to do good. Seek justice. Arrest oppressors. Defend orphans. Plead the case of widows." "Come on now, let's discuss this!" says the

LORD. "Though your sins are bright red, they will become as white as snow. Though they are dark red, they will become as white as wool."

Lamentation 3:8 (NKJV), "Even when I cry and shout, He shuts out my prayer."

Verse 44, "You have covered Yourself with a cloud, That prayer should not pass through."

Psalm 69:10-14 (ESV), "When I wept and humbled my soul with fasting, it became my reproach. When I made sackcloth my clothing, I became a byword to them. I am the talk of those who sit in the gate, and the drunkards make songs about me. But as for me, my prayer is to you, O Lord. At an acceptable time, O God, in the abundance of your steadfast love answer me in your saving faithfulness. Deliver me from sinking in the mire; let me be delivered from my enemies and from the deep waters."

Matthew 21:12-13 (GNT), "Jesus went into the Temple and drove out all those who were buying and selling there. He overturned the tables of the moneychangers and the stools of those who sold pigeons, and said to them, "It is written in the Scriptures that God said, 'My Temple will be called a house of prayer.' But you are making it a hideout for thieves!"

Daniel 9:2-7 (NLT) "During the first year of his reign, I, Daniel, learned from reading the word of the LORD, as revealed to Jeremiah the prophet, that Jerusalem must lie desolate for seventy years. So I turned to the Lord God and pleaded with him in prayer and fasting. I also wore rough burlap and sprinkled myself with ashes. I prayed to the LORD my God and confessed:

"O Lord, you are a great and awesome God! You always fulfill your covenant and keep your promises of unfailing love to those who love you and obey your commands. But we have sinned and done wrong. We have rebelled against you and scorned your commands and regulations. We have refused to listen to your servants the prophets, who spoke on your authority to our kings and princes and ancestors and to all the people of the land. "Lord, you are in the right; but as you see, our faces are covered with shame. This is true of all of us, including the people of Judah and

Jerusalem and all Israel, scattered near and far, wherever you have driven us because of our disloyalty to you"

Verses 20-23, "I went on praying and confessing my sin and the sin of my people, pleading with the LORD my God for Jerusalem, his holy mountain. As I was praying, Gabriel, whom I had seen in the earlier vision, came swiftly to me at the time of the evening sacrifice. He explained to me, "Daniel, I have come here to give you insight and understanding. The moment you began praying, a command was given. And now I am here to tell you what it was, for you are very precious to God. Listen carefully so that you can understand the meaning of your vision."

There is room for grace with God when the heart sincerely invites God, and humble itself in prayer in obedience to God. Humility to God that also reflects in humble relations to one another, as fellow humans.

James 4:5-10 (NIV), "Or do you think Scripture says without reason that he jealously longs for the spirit he has caused to dwell in us? But he gives us more grace. That is why Scripture says: "God opposes the proud but shows favor to the humble." Submit yourselves, then, to God. Resist the devil, and he will flee from you. Come near to God and he will come near to you. Wash your hands, you sinners, and purify your hearts, you double-minded. Grieve, mourn and wail. Change your laughter to mourning and your joy to gloom. Humble yourselves before the Lord, and he will lift you up."

James 5:16 (NLT), "Confess your sins to each other and pray for each other so that you may be healed. The earnest prayer of a righteous person has great power and produces wonderful results."

Matthew 5:23-24 (NIV), "Therefore, if you are offering your gift at the altar and there remember that your brother or sister has something against you, leave your gift there in front of the altar. First go and be reconciled to them; then come and offer your gift."

1 Peter 3:7 (ESV), "Likewise, husbands, live with your wives in an understanding way, showing honor to the woman as the weaker vessel, since they are heirs with you of the grace of life, so that your prayers may not be hindered."

1 Kings 8:28 (NIV), "Yet give attention to your servant's prayer and his plea for mercy, LORD my God. Hear the cry and the prayer that your servant is praying in your presence this day."

2 Chronicles 7:14 (ESV), "if my people who are called by my name humble themselves, and pray and seek my face and turn from their wicked ways, then I will hear from heaven and will forgive their sin and heal their land."

Psalms 119:165 (ISV) "Great peace belongs to those who love your instruction, and nothing makes them stumble."

Chapter Fourteen

POSTURES AND VOICE IN PRAYERS, BEFORE AND AFTER

- What scripture says on what posture you adopt in prayer is based mainly on individual preference, but more paramount is the fact that the heart must focus on God.

- God hears not because of a stance or volume of voice but sincerity of heart that is connected to His will. It's interesting to see though that one may clasp their hands together in prayer, another may lift their hands towards heaven, another fall flat on the ground or bow their head, or sit quietly in a corner, one may prefer to prayer walk and pace about. What becomes clear in time is whether any action was done in misplaced pride or self-aggrandisement, rather than giving glory to God.

- If you made a vow in this regard, then be prepared to fulfil it.

- However, on your own freewill you may adopt what helps you express reverence towards God.

Prophet Moses would see triumph as long as He held His hands up in reverence to God.

Exodus 17:9-13 (ESV), "So Moses said to Joshua, "Choose for us men, and go out and fight with Amalek. Tomorrow I will stand on the top of the hill with the staff of God in my hand." So Joshua did as Moses told him, and fought with Amalek, while Moses, Aaron, and Hur went up to the top of the hill. Whenever Moses held up his hand, Israel prevailed, and whenever he lowered his hand, Amalek prevailed. But Moses' hands grew weary, so they took a stone and put it under him, and he sat on it, while Aaron and Hur held up his hands, one on one side, and the other on the other side. So his hands were steady until the going down of the sun. And Joshua overwhelmed Amalek and his people with the sword."

King David would pray in this way-

Psalm 28:2 (NIV), "Hear my cry for mercy as I call to you for help, as I lift up my hands toward your Most Holy Place."

Psalm 95:6-7 (NIV), "Come, let us bow down in worship, let us kneel before the Lord our Maker; for he is our God and we are the people of his pasture, the flock under his care. Today, if only you would hear his voice"

Also, in 1 Kings 8:54-56 (CEV), "When Solomon finished his prayer at the altar, he was kneeling with his arms lifted toward heaven. He stood up, turned toward the people, blessed them, and said loudly: Praise the LORD! He has kept his promise and given us peace. Every good thing he promised to his servant Moses has happened."

How did Jesus respond to those who stood in prayer or came prostrate? He was more inclined to their intent, whether they are bent to look good as humble or actually being humble; quite a subtle difference which takes those paying attention and spirit-led to see.

Mark 11:25 (NKJV) "And whenever you stand praying, if you have anything against anyone, forgive him, that your Father in heaven may also forgive you your trespasses."

Matthew 6:5-8 (ESV) also says, "And when you pray, you must not be like the hypocrites. For they love to stand and pray in the synagogues and at the street corners, that they may be seen by others. Truly, I say to you, they have received their reward. But when you pray, go into your room and shut the door and pray to your Father who is in secret. And your Father who sees in secret will reward you. "And when you pray, do not heap up empty phrases as the Gentiles do, for they think that they will be heard for their many words. Do not be like them, for your Father knows what you need before you ask him."

Apostle Paul leaves us something to ruminate on, he suggests this attitude in prayer as a doctrine of reverence when praying or prophesying for a man in the Church.

1 Corinthians 11:2-4 (NLT), "I am so glad that you always keep me in your thoughts, and that you are following the teachings I passed on to you. But there is one thing I want you to know: The head of every man is Christ, the head of woman is man, and the head of Christ is God. A man dishonors his head if he covers his head while praying or prophesying."

1 Timothy 2:8 (NKJV), "I desire therefore that the men pray everywhere, lifting up holy hands, without wrath and doubting;"

Ezra also in the old testament would intercede in this manner,

Ezra 9:5-6 (NKJV) "At the evening sacrifice I arose from my fasting; and having torn my garment and my robe, I fell on my knees and spread out my hands to the Lord my God. And I said: "O my God, I am too ashamed and humiliated to lift up my face to You, my God; for our iniquities have risen higher than our heads, and our guilt has grown up to the heavens."

Also, 2 Kings 19:14 (NLT), "After Hezekiah received the letter from the messengers and read it, he went up to the LORD's Temple and spread it out before the LORD."

2 Samuel 12:15-24 (NIV) After Nathan had gone home, the Lord struck the child that Uriah's wife had borne to David, and he became ill. David pleaded with God for the child. He fasted and spent the nights lying in sackcloth on the ground. The elders of his household stood beside him to get him up from the ground, but he refused, and he would not eat any food with them. On the seventh day the child died. David's attendants were afraid to tell him that the child was dead, for they thought, "While the child was still living, he wouldn't listen to us when we spoke to him. How can we now tell him the child is dead? He may do something desperate." David noticed that his attendants were whispering among themselves, and he realized the child was dead. "Is the child dead?" he asked. "Yes," they replied, "he is dead." Then David got up from the ground. After he had washed, put on lotions and changed his clothes, he went into the house of the Lord and worshiped. Then he went to his own house, and at his request they served him food, and he ate. His attendants asked him, "Why are you acting this way? While the child was alive, you fasted and wept, but now that the child is dead, you get up and eat!" He answered, "While the child was still alive, I fasted and wept. I thought, 'Who knows? The Lord may be gracious to me and let the child live.' But now that he is dead, why should I go on fasting? Can I bring him back again? I will go to him, but he will not return to me." Then David comforted his wife Bathsheba, and he went to her and made love to her. She gave birth to a son, and they named him Solomon. The Lord loved him; and because the Lord loved him, he sent word through Nathan the prophet to name him Jedidiah."

1 Kings 18:42-43 (MSG), "Ahab did it: got up and ate and drank. Meanwhile, Elijah climbed to the top of Carmel, bowed deeply in prayer, his face between his knees. Then he said to his young servant, "On your feet now! Look toward the sea." He went, looked, and reported back, "I don't see a thing." "Keep looking," said Elijah, "seven times if necessary."
"

Lamentation 2:19 (CEV), "Get up and pray for help all through the night. Pour out your feelings to the Lord, as you would pour water out of a jug. Beg him to save your people, who are starving to death at every street crossing."

Let us consider the Lord,

John 11:40-44 (NLT), "Jesus responded, "Didn't I tell you that you would see God's glory if you believe?" So they rolled the stone aside. Then Jesus looked up to heaven and said, "Father, thank you for hearing me. You always hear me, but I said it out loud for the sake of all these people standing here, so that they will believe you sent me." Then Jesus shouted, "Lazarus, come out!" And the dead man came out, his hands and feet bound in graveclothes, his face wrapped in a headcloth. Jesus told them, "Unwrap him and let him go!" "

Luke 9:16 (GNT), "Jesus took the five loaves and two fish, looked up to heaven, thanked God for them, broke them, and gave them to the disciples to distribute to the people."

Luke 24:50-53 (CSB), "Then he led them out to the vicinity of Bethany, and lifting up his hands he blessed them. And while he was blessing them, he left them and was carried up into heaven. After worshiping him, they returned to Jerusalem with great joy. And they were continually in the temple praising God."

Deuteronomy 32:40-41 (NIV), "I lift my hand to heaven and solemnly swear: As surely as I live forever, when I sharpen my flashing sword and my hand grasps it in judgment, I will take vengeance on my adversaries and repay those who hate me."

Chapter Fifteen

HEAVEN'S DISCRETION

- It is God that hears prayers. The believer only talks to God in secret, but it is God that is able to make alive or bring to an end the evil doer and his or her works.
- Consider always in your dealings that sovereignty belongs to God. All power belongs to Him. If after praying your answers are delayed, do not fret, only remember who God is, because you as a person are not. Neither should any man or woman blame you for God's manner of justice or seeming absence of action.

Let's consider this verse in light of Christ being the Son of God and having authority to perform this spiritual function of baptism- he surely like John the Baptist could demonstrate that God intends to take away sins; but instead He instructs His disciples to do the baptisms, as news spread around of the revival and greater responses than John's ministry. Seen in John 4:2 (NKJV), "though Jesus himself didn't baptize them—his disciples did)". Similarly remember Christ authority to lay down or pick up His life. Through Scriptures we find it is the purpose of God that will stand.

It is God that appoints authority and pulls down. When it seems the purpose of man strives but for a moment, the purpose of God ultimately will thrive, and it will be evident in righteousness and the blessing of the Lord that God reigns. God establishes His reign if we trust Him. Even the seeming triumph of the wicked for a season is a fine opportunity to show His power and ultimately bring it to ridicule. There is glory in a pulling down of a stronghold.

Romans 9:14-24 (GNT) says, "Shall we say, then, that God is unjust? Not at all. For he said to Moses, "I will have mercy on anyone I wish; I will take pity on anyone I wish." So then, everything depends, not on what we humans want or do, but only on God's mercy. For the scripture says to the king of Egypt, "I made you king in order to use you to show my power and to spread my fame over the whole world." So then, God has mercy on anyone he wishes, and he makes stubborn anyone he wishes. But one of you will say to me, "If this is so, how can God find fault with anyone? Who can resist God's will?" But who are you, my friend, to talk back to God? A clay pot does not ask the man who made it, "Why did you make me like this?" After all, the man who makes the pots has the right to use the clay as he wishes, and to make two pots from the same lump of clay, one for special occasions and the other for ordinary use. And the same is true of what God has done. He wanted to show his anger and to make his power known. But he was very patient in enduring those who were the objects of his anger, who were doomed to destruction. And he also wanted to reveal his abundant glory, which was poured out on us who are the objects of his mercy, those of us whom he has prepared to receive his glory. For we are the people he called, not only from among the Jews but also from among the Gentiles."

Psalm 2:1-12 (GNT), "Why do the nations plan rebellion? Why do people make their useless plots? Their kings revolt, their rulers plot together against the Lord and against the king he chose. "Let us free ourselves from their rule," they say; "let us throw off their control." From his throne in heaven the Lord laughs and mocks their feeble plans. Then he warns them in anger and terrifies them with his fury. "On Zion, my sacred hill," he says, "I have installed my king." "I will announce," says the king, "what the Lord has declared. He said to me: 'You are my son; today I have become your father. Ask, and I will give you all the nations; the whole earth will be yours. You will break them with an iron rod; you will shatter them in pieces like a clay pot.'" Now listen to this warning, you kings; learn this lesson, you rulers of the world: Serve the Lord with fear; tremble and bow down to him; or else his anger will be quickly aroused, and you will suddenly die. Happy are all who go to him for protection."

Consider the move of God amongst the disciples, whilst they prayed normally the power of God was affecting the earthly elements causing a shaking, in Acts 4:31-33 (NIV) "After they prayed, the place where they were meeting was shaken. And they were all filled with the Holy Spirit and spoke the word of God boldly. All the believers were one in heart and mind. No one claimed that any of their possessions was their own, but they shared everything they had. With great power the apostles continued to testify to the resurrection of the Lord Jesus. And God's grace was so powerfully at work in them all"

What did Jesus say in John 5:30 (NIV), "By myself I can do nothing; I judge only as I hear, and my judgment is just, for I seek not to please myself but him who sent me."

HEART AND MOUTH, EAR AND EYES IN PRAYER

- The connection between these 'parts' do matter. This is because words can be empty if not sincere and heartfelt. God on this other side of the Xray machine can see the foreign object in the heart that should be outside. A prayer for vengeance on the innocent would fall on deaf ears, His eyes would see their affliction and hear their prayers instead.

- Pray instead to see God's will, to hear His voice, for your heart to beat at His pause, and that your mouth may speak His will. Not that which as a human you may crave, but that which glorifies God.

The prophetic word is to align with the purpose of God- that will be intelligence that endures and truly flourishes. The wisdom of God to choose God, to trust Him, to talk to Him about your cares and ask Him to help lead you into the pathway of your destiny, that will bring you joy and healing. This begins by truly opening your heart to God.

Isaiah 29:13-14 (NIV), "The Lord says: "These people come near to me with their mouth and honor me with their lips, but their hearts are far from me. Their worship of me is based on merely human rules they have been taught. Therefore once more I will astound these people with wonder upon wonder; the wisdom of the wise will perish, the intelligence of the intelligent will vanish."

Daniel 11:30-32 (KJV), "For the ships of Chittim shall come against him: therefore he shall be grieved, and return, and have indignation against the holy covenant: so shall he do; he shall even return, and have intelligence with them that forsake the holy covenant. And arms shall stand on his part, and they shall pollute the sanctuary of strength, and shall take away the daily sacrifice, and they shall place the abomination that maketh desolate. And such as do wickedly against the covenant shall he corrupt by flatteries: but the people that do know their God shall be strong, and do exploits"

Psalm 51:17 (CEV), "The way to please you is to be truly sorry deep in our hearts. This is the kind of sacrifice you won't refuse."

Psalm 17:1 (NLT), "O LORD, hear my plea for justice. Listen to my cry for help. Pay attention to my prayer, for it comes from honest lips."

Psalm 54:2 (NKJV), "Hear my prayer, O God; Give ear to the words of my mouth"

Psalm 64:1 (NLT), "O God, listen to my complaint. Protect my life from my enemies' threats."

God warns against insincere prayers.

Matthew 23:14 (NKJV), "Woe to you, scribes and Pharisees, hypocrites! For you devour widows' houses, and for a pretense make long prayers. Therefore you will receive greater condemnation."

Also pray for spiritual sight to see. For instance, in the natural you may see a conflict or difficult job or impossible marriage, but if you pray God may show you why you need to be patient, that He will make a way.

Acts 11:5 (NASB), "I was in the city of Joppa praying; and in a trance I saw a vision, an object coming down like a great sheet lowered by four corners from the sky; and it came right down to me,

2 Kings 6:17 (GNT), "Then he prayed, "O LORD, open his eyes and let him see!" The LORD answered his prayer, and Elisha's servant looked up and saw the hillside covered with horses and chariots of fire all around Elisha."

Chapter Seventeen

TALKING TO GOD NOT MAN: CONVERSATIONS IN PRAYER

- God is calling us to recalibrate our prayer lifestyle in the face of Jesus.

- A prayer not based on gossip, or one to get even, but rather as though no one else needs an ear- focusing your conversation principally to God.

- If you are in a group praying in turns, you may use your chance to rip another in parables and innuendos whilst maintaining a straight face, or you could choose to raise a honest intercession- and make sure the whole time your focus is on God who you talk to. Else it would be like talking with your spouse while on a lovely walk together whilst the whole time walking sideways and talking to a stranger on the path. Most people would consider that out of step and bordering on awkward.

- You may find you inspire others in your praying, but if you have no desire to communicate to God, or have confidence that you speak to God alone, then there is no purpose of spiritually effective prayer; because your answer is to come from God not man. If your aim is to speak in wisdom or request from your neighbour by stealth, that effectively achieves another goal.

Consider a prayer that puts God as the centre of focus-

Psalm 65:2 (NKJV), "O You who hear prayer, To You all flesh will come."

Psalm 141:2 (NLT) "Accept my prayer as incense offered to you, and my upraised hands as an evening offering."

1 Kings 8:54 (GNT), "After Solomon had finished praying to the LORD, he stood up in front of the altar, where he had been kneeling with uplifted hands."

John's vision in Revelations 5:8 (ESV), "And between the throne and the four living creatures and among the elders I saw a Lamb standing, as though it had been slain, with seven horns and with seven eyes, which are the seven spirits of God sent out into all the earth. And he went and took the scroll from the right hand of him who was seated on the throne. And when he had taken the scroll, the four living creatures and the twenty-four elders fell down before the Lamb, each holding a harp, and golden bowls full of incense, which are the prayers of the saints. And they sang a new song, saying, "Worthy are you to take the scroll and to open its seals, for you were slain, and by your blood you ransomed people for God from every tribe and language and people and nation, and you have made them a kingdom and priests to our God, and they shall reign on the earth."

Revelations 8:2-4 (ERV), "And I saw the seven angels which stand before God; and there were given unto them seven trumpets. And another angel came and stood over the altar, having a golden censer; and there was given unto him much incense, that he should add it unto the prayers of all the saints upon the golden altar which was before the throne. And the smoke of the incense, with the prayers of the saints, went up before God out of the angel's hand."

God's intent is to restore His grace, and enable His glory to be seen, this is because a prayer that focuses on God takes discipline and faithfulness in your conversation. It requires hard work with discipline and reverence to focus the mind away from flying spaghettis or silly imageries, to what matters- the cross of Christ. The mind may seek to wander, but part of spiritual warfare is to discern rightly and bringing it in conformity to the knowledge of God. In Christ's name, direct your mind to sit down at the foot of the cross, where the peace and love of God overwhelms you, any look continually into spiritual eyes of God's grace and truth.

2 Corinthians 10:2-3 (NIV) tells us, "The weapons we fight with are not the weapons of the world. On the contrary, they have divine power to demolish strongholds. We demolish arguments and every pretension that sets itself up against the knowledge of God, and we take captive every thought to make it obedient to Christ."

Isaiah 1:26 (NASB), "Then I will restore your judges as at the first, and your counselors as at the beginning; After that you will be called the city of righteousness, A faithful city."

Daniel 9:20-24 (NIV), "While I was speaking and praying, confessing my sin and the sin of my people Israel and making my request to the Lord my God for his holy hill— while I was still in prayer, Gabriel, the man I had seen in the earlier vision, came to me in swift flight about the time of the evening sacrifice. He instructed me and said to me, "Daniel, I have now come to give you insight and understanding. As soon as you began to pray, a word went out, which I have come to tell you, for you are highly esteemed. Therefore, consider the word and understand the vision: "Seventy 'sevens' are decreed for your people and your holy city to finish transgression, to put an end to sin, to atone for wickedness, to bring in everlasting righteousness, to seal up vision and prophecy and to anoint the Most Holy Place"

Ephesians 6:17-18 (NLT), "Put on salvation as your helmet, and take the sword of the Spirit, which is the word of God. Pray in the Spirit at all times and on every occasion. Stay alert and be persistent in your prayers for all believers everywhere"

Chapter Eighteen

TEARS AND JOYS OF PERSEVERANCE IN PRAYER

- You may be lost for words, but your tears speak.
- God considers labours in prayers.

You can find God's comfort in the scriptures. Tears is no weakness, because there are times the troubles in life makes you cry- but remember to pray in those tears. If God permits, there are things you see that could touch your heart, and suffering of others that move you to action, even maybe persecution that ostracise and hurt you badly, your tears become a prayer that speaks for God's justice and change towards heaven's blessings. See-

Lamentation 3:48-50 (ISV), "My eyes run with rivers of tears over the destruction of my cherished people. My tears pour down ceaselessly; I am far from relief until the LORD bends down to see from heaven."

Psalm 56:8 (NLT), "You keep track of all my sorrows. You have collected all my tears in your bottle. You have recorded each one in your book."

Psalm 39:12 (GWT), "Listen to my prayer, O LORD. Open your ear to my cry for help. Do not be deaf to my tears, for I am a foreign resident with you, a stranger like all my ancestors."

Romans 12:12 (ESV), "Rejoice in hope, be patient in tribulation, be constant in prayer."

Hebrews 5:5-10 (ERV), "So Christ also glorified not himself to be made a high priest, but he that spake unto him, Thou art my Son, This day have I begotten thee: as he saith also in another place, Thou art a priest for ever After the order of Melchizedek. Who in the days of his flesh, having offered up prayers and supplications with strong crying and tears unto him that was able to save him from death, and having been heard for his godly fear, though he was a Son, yet learned obedience by the things which he suffered; and having been made perfect, he became unto all them that obey him the author of eternal salvation; named of God a high priest after the order of Melchizedek."

1 Thessalonian 5:16-18 (NLT), "Always be joyful. Never stop praying. Be thankful in all circumstances, for this is God's will for you who belong to Christ Jesus."

Consider God's word to Hezekiah through Prophet Isaiah in a time of sickness,

Isaiah 38:5 (NLT), "Go back to Hezekiah and tell him, 'This is what the LORD, the God of your ancestor David, says: I have heard your prayer and seen your tears. I will add fifteen years to your life"

Also we can consider the Lord Christ as he ministered to Lazarus, in John 11: 33-44 (NIV), "When Mary reached the place where Jesus was and saw him, she fell at his feet and said, "Lord, if you had been here, my brother would not have died." When Jesus saw her weeping, and the Jews who had come along with her also weeping, he was deeply moved in spirit and troubled. "Where have you laid him?" he asked. "Come and see, Lord," they replied. Jesus wept. Then the Jews said, "See how he loved him!" But some of them said, "Could not he who opened the eyes of the blind man have kept this man from dying?" Jesus, once more deeply moved, came to the tomb. It was a cave with a stone laid across the entrance. "Take away the stone," he said. "But, Lord," said Martha, the sister of the dead man, "by this time there is a bad odor, for he has been there four days." Then

Jesus said, "Did I not tell you that if you believe, you will see the glory of God?" So they took away the stone. Then Jesus looked up and said, "Father, I thank you that you have heard me. I knew that you always hear me, but I said this for the benefit of the people standing here, that they may believe that you sent me." When he had said this, Jesus called in a loud voice, "Lazarus, come out!" The dead man came out, his hands and feet wrapped with strips of linen, and a cloth around his face. Jesus said to them, "Take off the grave clothes and let him go."

To a priest of God named Zechariah whose family needed a child, God's victory is shown in response to their prayer-

Luke 1:5-17 (NIV), "In the time of Herod king of Judea there was a priest named Zechariah, who belonged to the priestly division of Abijah; his wife Elizabeth was also a descendant of Aaron. Both of them were righteous in the sight of God, observing all the Lord's commands and decrees blamelessly. But they were childless because Elizabeth was not able to conceive, and they were both very old. Once when Zechariah's division was on duty and he was serving as priest before God, he was chosen by lot, according to the custom of the priesthood, to go into the temple of the Lord and burn incense. And when the time for the burning of incense came, all the assembled worshipers were praying outside. Then an angel of the Lord appeared to him, standing at the right side of the altar of incense. When Zechariah saw him, he was startled and was gripped with fear. But the angel said to him: "Do not be afraid, Zechariah; your prayer has been heard. Your wife Elizabeth will bear you a son, and you are to call him John. He will be a joy and delight to you, and many will rejoice because of his birth, for he will be great in the sight of the Lord. He is never to take wine or other fermented drink, and he will be filled with the Holy Spirit even before he is born. He will bring back many of the people of Israel to the Lord their God. And he will go on before the Lord, in the spirit and power of Elijah, to turn the hearts of the parents to their children and the disobedient to the wisdom of the righteous—to make ready a people prepared for the Lord."

Also in Acts 10:30-36 (NKJV), "So Cornelius said, "Four days ago I was fasting until this hour; and at the ninth hour I prayed in my house, and behold, a man stood before me in bright clothing, and said, 'Cornelius, your prayer has been heard, and your alms are remembered in the sight of God. Send therefore to Joppa and call Simon here, whose surname is Peter. He is lodging in the house of Simon, a tanner, by the sea. When he comes, he will speak to you.' So I sent to you immediately, and you have done well to come. Now therefore, we are all present before God, to hear all the things commanded you by God." Then Peter opened his mouth and said: "In truth I perceive that God shows no partiality. But in every nation whoever fears Him and works righteousness is accepted by Him. The word which God sent to the children of Israel, preaching peace through Jesus Christ—He is Lord of all"

Chapter Nineteen

WAITING TIME

- After praying, have the tenacity to wait on God for answer. It is like at a restaurant after ordering a meal you wait for it to be prepared and presented. You may have the right to flare up after a minute, but what is the point. Spiritually, God is a bit the same, He may take minutes, hours, even months or years – but I urge you to wait, because even though you placed an order for steak if you have no teeth and still growing as a baby, He may serve you milk and put your request for meat on a later date, even if on a voucher. The illustration is to say God knows better. Only wait.

- Waiting requires the skill of patience, not killing time but managing it wisely in anticipation of the worth of return. It is a fruit of the Spirit. It also is like being placed on a high priority list to dine with a King, you cherish the honour and preserve it till the appointed time. If you make wise investments and use time well it would produce good results.

Ecclesiastics 11:1 (NLT) says, "Send your grain across the seas, and in time, profits will flow back to you"

As you trust the Lord for increase patiently, God will hear and respond to your prayer, seeing your sustained faith.

In Psalm 27:13-14 (ERV), "I had fainted, unless I had believed to see the goodness of the LORD in the land of the living. Wait on the LORD: be strong, and let thine heart take courage; yea, wait thou on the LORD."

Isaiah 40:28-31 (ESV), "He gives power to the faint, and to him who has no might he increases strength. Even youths shall faint and be weary, and young men shall fall exhausted; but they who wait for the Lord shall renew their strength; they shall mount up with wings like eagles; they shall run and not be weary; they shall walk and not faint."

Luke 24:49 (GNT), "And I myself will send upon you what my Father has promised. But you must wait in the city until the power from above comes down upon you."

Christ Himself made a choice to wait on God and take time to make important decisions. Don't be disheartened if your pick turns out not too well, or your hard work don't churn out much profit, be encouraged because if God gave you an approval at the start it will make sense in the end- God makes all things work out for good.

Luke 6:12-16 (NKJV), "Now it came to pass in those days that He went out to the mountain to pray, and continued all night in prayer to God. And when it was day, He called His disciples to Himself; and from them He chose twelve whom He also named apostles: Simon, whom He also named Peter, and Andrew his brother; James and John; Philip and Bartholomew; Matthew and Thomas; James the son of Alphaeus, and Simon called the Zealot; Judas the son of James, and Judas Iscariot who also became a traitor."

Also in Daniel 9:23 (GWT) we see God sent His Angel to say He heard all Daniel's prayers, and that in fact we see the willingness of God to hear and answer, so we can trust His timing- "As soon as you began to make your request, a reply was sent. I have come to give you the reply because you are highly respected. So study the message, and understand the vision"

Let us consider Simeon and Anna- their story shows how long they waited, praying daily in the temple waiting for a divine visitation. Waiting to see the messiah- such incredible faith. They heard clearly, they had a deep assurance of a good God able to answer.

Luke 2:25-35 (CEV), "At this time a man named Simeon was living in Jerusalem. Simeon was a good man. He loved God and was waiting for him to save the people of Israel. God's Spirit came to him and told him that he would not die until he had seen Christ the Lord. When Mary and Joseph brought Jesus to the temple to do what the Law of Moses says should be done for a new baby, the Spirit told Simeon to go into the temple. Simeon took the baby Jesus in his arms and praised God, "Lord, I am your servant, and now I can die in peace, because you have kept your promise to me. With my own eyes I have seen what you have done to save your people, and foreign nations will also see this. Your mighty power is a light for all nations, and it will bring honor to your people Israel." Jesus' parents were surprised at what Simeon had said. Then he blessed them and told Mary, "This child of yours will cause many people in Israel to fall and others to stand. The child will be like a warning sign. Many people will reject him, and you, Mary, will suffer as though you had been stabbed by a dagger. But all this will show what people are really thinking."

The prophet Anna was also there in the temple. She was the daughter of Phanuel from the tribe of Asher, and she was very old. In her youth she had been married for seven years, but her husband died. And now she was 84 years old. Night and day she served God in the temple by praying and often going without eating. At this time Anna came in and praised God. She spoke about the child Jesus to everyone who hoped for Jerusalem to be set free."

Chapter Twenty

EXPECTATIONS TO RECEIVE

- When you pray expect answers; this is lifting and exercising your faith.

- Righteousness is not enough if no expectation to receive, except if God acts in His mercy. God still reserves the discretion to place a hold. Often God would work mightily in response to our belief not unbelief.

Apostle Paul would write to Philemon, as well as Apphia and Archippus, and other believers who hold Christian meetings in his house, encouraging them in the faith and reassuring them of a visit in expectation of answer to his prayers. Philemon 1:21-22 (NLT), "am confident as I write this letter that you will do what I ask and even more! One more thing—please prepare a guest room for me, for I am hoping that God will answer your prayers and let me return to you soon."

Solomon held God to His promise to his Father, expecting a fulfilment in 1 Kings 8:26 (ESV), "Now therefore, O God of Israel, let your word be confirmed, which you have spoken to your servant David my father."

Consider Johanan and those all who sought counsel from Prophet Jeremiah, seeking direction from the Lord. However, though they did well to expect answers (guidance), but we see a reluctance to comply in the end when the answers came. God is teaching His people to be open minded to the Spirit, in being able to receive but also utilise rightly.

Jeremiah 42:1-22 (NIV) "Then all the army officers, including Johanan son of Kareah and Jezaniah son of Hoshaiah, and all the people from the least to the greatest approached Jeremiah the prophet and said to him, "Please hear our petition and pray to the Lord your God for this entire remnant. For as you now see, though we were once many, now only a few are left. Pray that the Lord your God will tell us where we should go and what we should do." "I have heard you," replied Jeremiah the prophet. "I will certainly pray to the Lord your God as you have requested; I will tell you everything the Lord says and will keep nothing back from you."

Then they said to Jeremiah, "May the Lord be a true and faithful witness against us if we do not act in accordance with everything the Lord your God sends you to tell us. Whether it is favorable or unfavorable, we will obey the Lord our God, to whom we are sending you, so that it will go well with us, for we will obey the Lord our God." Ten days later the word of the Lord came to Jeremiah. So he called together Johanan son of Kareah and all the army officers who were with him and all the people from the least to the greatest. He said to them, "This is what the Lord, the God of Israel, to whom you sent me to present your petition, says: 'If you stay in this land, I will build you up and not tear you down; I will plant you and not uproot you, for I have relented concerning the disaster I have inflicted on you. Do not be afraid of the king of Babylon, whom you now fear. Do not be afraid of him, declares the Lord, for I am with you and will save you and deliver you from his hands. I will show you compassion so that he will have compassion on you and restore you to your land.'

"However, if you say, 'We will not stay in this land,' and so disobey the Lord your God, and if you say, 'No, we will go and live in Egypt, where we will not see war or hear the trumpet or be hungry for bread,' then hear the word of the Lord, you remnant of Judah. This is what the Lord Almighty, the God of Israel, says: 'If you are determined to go to Egypt and you do go to settle there, then the sword you fear will overtake you there, and the famine you dread will follow you into Egypt, and there you will die. Indeed, all who are determined to go to Egypt to settle there will die by the sword, famine and plague; not one of them will survive or escape the disaster I will bring on them.' This is what the Lord Almighty, the God of Israel, says: 'As my anger and wrath have been poured out on those who lived in Jerusalem, so will my wrath be poured out on you when you go to Egypt. You will be a curse and an object of horror, a curse and an object of reproach; you will never see this place again.'

"Remnant of Judah, the Lord has told you, 'Do not go to Egypt.' Be sure of this: I warn you today that you made a fatal mistake when you sent me to the Lord your God and said, 'Pray to the Lord our God for us; tell us everything he says and we will do it.' I have told you today, but you still have not obeyed the Lord your God in all he sent me to tell you. So now, be sure of this: You will die by the sword, famine and plague in the place where you want to go to settle."

Christ reminds us that our expectations must also match with God's overall plan, a call to sacrificial living, to seek more the perfect will of God than a permissive trajectory. You can see this principle in Matthew 26:53 (NLT) His question in the presence of those seeking His arrest and His disciple's resistance, "Don't you realize that I could ask my Father for thousands of angels to protect us, and he would send them instantly? But if I did, how would the Scriptures be fulfilled that describe what must happen now?"

Mark 11:22-24 (ESV), "And Jesus answered them, "Have faith in God. Truly, I say to you, whoever says to this mountain, 'Be taken up and thrown into the sea,' and does not doubt in his heart, but believes that what he says will come to pass, it will be done for him. Therefore I tell you, whatever you ask in prayer, believe that you have received it, and it will be yours"

Chapter Twenty-One

LEARNING THE ACT OF PRAYER

- Consider it necessary to 'learn' to pray, like every true disciple.

- Christ taught us to pray, so we can reflect on each element of Matthew 6:5-15; focus on the secret condition of your heart than the public praise, seek to glorify God and pray His purpose stand, also remember to make your requests known with contentment, and be gracious in your hearts as God has been to you. When you pray individually, Christ suggests talking to God as though He alone hears you, shut out every distractions, and then pray. To live in heaven's kind of peace and blessing consider Matthew 5:1-11, 23-26; come to God with peace in your heart and let God's peace rule your thoughts.

- It is possible to nourish the soul with truth and make the Spirit's power effective through prayer.

- Consider using this incredible gift of prayer and constantly exercising it.

Within your grasp is the opportunity to pray better. That is what this whole book is about- apart from emphasing the need to pray and God's given doctrine or instruction, knowing you can learn to pray and how is important.

Luke 11:1-2 (ESV), "Now Jesus was praying in a certain place, and when he finished, one of his disciples said to him, "Lord, teach us to pray, as John taught his disciples." And he said to them, "When you pray, say: "Father, hallowed be your name. Your kingdom come.""

2 Peter 3:18 (NLT), "Rather, you must grow in the grace and knowledge of our Lord and Savior Jesus Christ. All glory to him, both now and forever! Amen."

1 Peter 2:2 (GNT), "Be like newborn babies, always thirsty for the pure spiritual milk, so that by drinking it you may grow up and be saved."

Prayer is not a way to be absolved of attending to practical necessities within your power. If God has supplied the means, then be an answer to another's need, perhaps they had sought the Lord, and He brought you their way. It is well within place to ask for the Lord to enable you further. Prayer is not an opportunity for the mockery of the principles of faith.

1 John 3:17-23 (GNT), "If we are rich and see others in need, yet close our hearts against them, how can we claim that we love God? My children, our love should not be just words and talk; it must be true love, which shows itself in action. This, then, is how we will know that we belong to the truth; this is how we will be confident in God's presence. If our conscience condemns us, we know that God is greater than our conscience and that he knows everything. And so, my dear friends, if our conscience does not condemn us, we have courage in God's presence. We receive from him whatever we ask, because we obey his commands and do what pleases him. What he commands is that we believe in his Son Jesus Christ and love one another, just as Christ commanded us."

James 2:14-19 (CEV), "My friends, what good is it to say you have faith, when you don't do anything to show you really do have faith? Can this kind of faith save you? If you know someone who doesn't have any clothes or food, you shouldn't just say, "I hope all goes well for you. I hope you will be warm and have plenty to eat." What good is it to say this, unless you do something to help? Faith that doesn't lead us to do good deeds is all alone and dead! Suppose someone disagrees and says, "It is possible to have faith without doing kind deeds." I would answer, "Prove that you have faith without doing kind deeds, and I will prove that I have faith by doing them." You surely believe there is only one God. That's fine. Even demons believe this, and it makes them shake with fear."

Consider a manner of prayer that acknowledges the work of Christ in you and through you, also along with other believers. Every good work God is doing in you includes others. Apostle Paul's example is to reach out to others in prayers, and encourage a caring community. Recently how has your prayers extended beyond self, and taken into context an acknowledgement of what God is positively doing already in another?

Philemon 4:8 (NKJV), "I thank my God, making mention of you always in my prayers, hearing of your love and faith which you have toward the Lord Jesus and toward all the saints, that the sharing of your faith may become effective by the acknowledgment of every good thing which is in you in Christ Jesus. For we have great joy and consolation in your love, because the hearts of the saints have been refreshed by you, brother."

Hebrews 10:25 (NLT) "And let us not neglect our meeting together, as some people do, but encourage one another, especially now that the day of his return is drawing near."

Colossians 3:15 (NLT), "And let the peace that comes from Christ rule in your hearts. For as members of one body you are called to live in peace. And always be thankful."

The word of God has the capability to produce knowledge that will make you wise in praying. So what do you want to pray about- opportunity to destroy the innocent, to steal from another, to bear false witness, to paint the wicked as deserving and the righteous as weak, to mock the option of praying and to praise self? Your conscience may prick you, but the bible will make clear such prayers are foolishness laden and not effective.

2 Timothy 3:15 (NKJV), "But you must continue in the things which you have learned and been assured of, knowing from whom you have learned them, and that from childhood you have known the Holy Scriptures, which are able to make you wise for salvation through faith which is in Christ Jesus."

Psalm 25:4 (ESV), "Make me to know your ways, O LORD; teach me your paths."

Psalm 143:10 (NLT), "Teach me to do your will, for you are my God. May your gracious Spirit lead me forward on a firm footing."

Psalm 86:11 (ISV), "Teach me your ways, LORD, that I may walk in your truth; let me wholeheartedly revere your name."

James 4:3 (NLV), "Or if you do ask, you do not receive because your reasons for asking are wrong. You want these things only to please yourselves."

Chapter Twenty-Two

CONSIDER SEVEN POINTS OF PRAYER

- There are some points of need to pray for:

  Healing;

  Favour and creativity for honest gain;

  Power to reap and fulfil destiny;

  Protection;

  Family and society;

  Spiritual graces;

  Credible influence and leadership to affect lives positively.

[If you can now, as you read, take some time to pray about these things- as you take the time to speak your bible inspired wishes to an invisible being, creator God, trust He hears you and that you are not just blabbing into thin air. Do this believing in God's ability to answer, to calm your heart, to direct you to information and people that will help you, to move things supernaturally in your favour, and to enable you to make wise choices, and for grace to acknowledge Him in the end of it all. Be ready to listen to God's prompt in your heart and through His word. I pray that your life be used for God's praise on the earth, Amen.]

- Prayer is a channel for receiving these things, this is because with regard to all of these things, you recognise it is in prayer you ask God and He grants them, and may even exceeds your need. What a testimony to the goodness of God when there is a response after a heartfelt conversation. Who questions God's sovereign discretion to heal a sick mind, or to raise the meek and lowly to place them in authority, and to bring the displaced and isolated into reckoning?
- Prayer moves the heart of God to redemptive action, so talk to Him, the creator of the heavens and earth.

God is actively minded to responding to prayers, so consider pouring your hearts out in confidence about any specific issue.

Philippians 4:5-7 (NKJV), "Be anxious for nothing, but in everything by prayer and supplication, with thanksgiving, let your requests be made known to God; 7and the peace of God, which surpasses all understanding, will guard your hearts and minds through Christ Jesus."

3 John 1:2 (NIV), "Dear friend, I pray that you may enjoy good health and that all may go well with you, even as your soul is getting along well."

Daniel 10:12 (ESV), "Then he said to me, "Fear not, Daniel, for from the first day that you set your heart to understand and humbled yourself before your God, your words have been heard, and I have come because of your words."

Acts 10:30-33 (NKJV), "So Cornelius said, "Four days ago I was fasting until this hour; and at the ninth hour I prayed in my house, and behold, a man stood before me in bright clothing, and said, 'Cornelius, your prayer has been heard, and your alms are remembered in the sight of God. Send therefore to Joppa and call Simon here, whose surname is Peter. He is lodging in the house of Simon, a tanner, by the sea. When he comes, he will speak to you.' So I sent to you immediately, and you have done well to come. Now therefore, we are all present before God, to hear all the things commanded you by God."

Psalm 51:17 (NIV), "My sacrifice, O God, is a broken spirit; a broken and contrite heart you, God, will not despise."

Chapter Twenty-Three

UNIFIED CONGREGATIONAL PRAYER

- God calls us to pray as a fellowship, together in harmony, each pouring their hearts in worship, coordinated and uncoordinated- but decently and in order. Prayer can be complicated but need not be, as it may require the dexterity of the hands a surgeon and a fierce compassion of a mother for her sick child. It is knowing when to do what, when to enjoy each blend of unison of a single musical instrument, and each blend of accompaniment, for a beautiful masterpiece. By 'coordinated' I mean from a single script of prayer, saying the words in unison; as this can be a powerful expression of unity of mind, though not necessary if those involved don't believe it- it becomes lip-service. But in agreement of the minds and lips it becomes something powerful to explore. Also, in 'uncoordinated' form, is releasing believers in a group to pick a single theme or request to God, and then pray in unity but in their own manner of expression, allowing each person to bear their soul to God on the matter, each so consumed in their heartfelt plea to God that they are almost immune to eavesdropping- and such that there will be absolutely no need for it. If peradventure your ears fall on another's words it would not be a distraction where all are praying honestly and collectively, but reminds you while the more you need to refocus on being more intentional about your own prayer, individually to God alongside others as they do same, you may even find some affirming connections as you trust God's Spirit. There can be a basis of the exercise faith to this practice, that God is omnipresent, omnipotent and omniscient, so He can attend to all prayer everywhere at once with viable answers. He is not distracted by a prayer in New York or one in Paris, or London, or of many gathered in a room. And also that God is not bi-polarised in His ability and fixated on one person to the exclusion of other activity- so none should worry about the seemingly uncoordinated nature but rather the grace of God revealed in the diverse yet true nature; that one can kneel, another stand, another lie flat, speaking in their dialects or in spiritual languages inspired by the spirit of faith, creating a climate of spiritual intensity of passion and disciplined conversation towards God, often almost like an Acts-2 experience of freedom of reverence in prayer. Where also a point is raised in prayer, for instance it is seeking God for rain on a dry patched earth, where each can use their local dialect, intelligence, temperament, to talk to God about the matter, without feeling foisted to a text or character. Some may stand, some may knee, some may lift their hands, each however speaking to God on an issue, or whatever points that may have been raised- there will be hardly room for the temptations of passive gossip as in a group listening to each other, taking turns. Each way can be effective, depending how it is used.

- We find examples in the bible of scripted prayers for the congregation, and spirit-inspired and biblically conformist collective prayers.

- The power of collective prayer is seen not only in the example of a Church as a group uniting in agreement, but also in an immediate family coming to God in agreement. There is something powerful when a man and a woman, as a married couple, or alongside their children, or with friends, pray about an issue before God. The bible points out their prayer could be hindered if the husband is not in agreement, arguing with his wife. It is as though God expects they come before Him bound in heart about their plea and worship, else their dispute would send up a distasteful fragrance- Apostle Peter explains this is why many prayers are not answered [1 Peter 3:7-9]. Jesus also recommends reconciliation with a friend or member of a congregation should precede giving a spiritual offering. This I believe is true for a family in collective prayer [Matthew 5:24].

Matthew 18:19-20 (AMP) says, "Again I say to you, that if two believers on earth agree [that is, are of one mind, in harmony] about anything that they ask [within the will of God], it will be done for them by My Father in heaven. For where two or three are gathered in My name [meeting together as My followers], I am there among them."

In Acts 1:12-17 (MSG) the disciples of Christ gathered to pray and meditate on the scriptures as a group, after Jesus's resurrection and ascension, "So they left the mountain called Olives and returned to Jerusalem. It was a little over half a mile. They went to the upper room they had been using as a meeting place: Peter, John, James, Andrew, Philip, Thomas, Bartholomew, Matthew, James, son of Alphaeus, Simon the Zealot, Judas, son of James. They agreed they were in this for good, completely together in prayer, the women included. Also Jesus' mother, Mary, and his brothers. During this time, Peter stood up in the company—there were about 120 of them in the room at the time—and said, "Friends, long ago the Holy Spirit spoke through David regarding Judas, who became the guide to those who arrested Jesus. That Scripture had to be fulfilled, and now has been. Judas was one of us and had his assigned place in this ministry."

I would share with you the story of the early Church and how they prayed together, and saw a mighty move of God in response:

Acts 4:18-31 (NKJV), "So they called them and commanded them not to speak at all nor teach in the name of Jesus. But Peter and John answered and said to them, "Whether it is right in the sight of God to listen to you more than to God, you judge. For we cannot but speak the things which we have seen and heard." So when they had further threatened them, they let them go, finding no way of punishing them, because of the people, since they all glorified God for what had been done. For the man was over forty years old on whom this miracle of healing had been performed. And being let go, they went to their own companions and reported all that the chief priests and elders had said to them. So when they heard that, they raised their voice to God with one accord and said: "Lord, You are God, who made heaven and earth and the sea, and all that is in them, who by the mouth of Your servant David have said: 'Why did the nations rage, And the people plot vain things? The kings of the earth took their stand, And the rulers were gathered together against the Lord and against His Christ.' "For truly against Your holy Servant Jesus, whom You anointed, both Herod and Pontius Pilate, with the Gentiles and the people of Israel, were gathered together to do whatever Your hand and Your purpose determined before to be done. Now, Lord, look on their threats, and grant to Your servants that with all boldness they may speak Your word, by stretching out Your hand to heal, and that signs and wonders may be done through the name of Your holy Servant Jesus." And when they had prayed, the place where they were assembled together was shaken; and they were all filled with the Holy Spirit, and they spoke the word of God with boldness."

Chapter Twenty-Four

A CONSECRATED PLACE OF PRAYER- THE POTENCY

- There is relevance in setting apart a place, a portion of space, perhaps temporarily or better still for a longer period time, for prayer.

- A recognition that in this place I learn to discipline myself to commune with God. When believers come together to raise a structure for such a purpose it is called Church, a house for God; in setting apart that space, we bless and consecrate it to the Lord, this becomes an act of reverence, an act of worship, which God delights in. Being in the presence of God causes darkness to flee, but it has to be in a place that honours God, not consecrated to devils or idolatry, then it's just blocks- it is the Spirit of God that brings freedom.

The Lord recognised the temple as a place of prayer. Though He prayed in the mountain- a quiet place, in the garden of Gethsemane, for the healing of many on the streets and in their homes, even outside a tomb; nonetheless He recognised the consecrated building, a place built and separated to God for prayer. To say God has discountenanced His house is to be operating in ignorance and suppressing the truth. The believer is part of the body of Christ, and his body the temple of Christ, and Christ spoke of His body as the temple of the Lord, in reference to the spiritual understanding, but physically God has a respect to His house, and there is a nexus between the Spirit and the body. God has regard to His house, we should as well. However, the Spirit takes pre-eminence over the physical because it is eternal, and truly is glorifying to God. But make no mistake to not esteem God's house.

Christ in Luke 18:9-10 (NIV) talks about going to the temple- "To some who were confident of their own righteousness and looked down on everyone else, Jesus told this parable: "Two men went up to the temple to pray, one a Pharisee and the other a tax collector."

Mark 11:15-19 (CSB), "They came to Jerusalem, and he went into the temple and began to throw out those buying and selling. He overturned the tables of the money changers and the chairs of those selling doves, and would not permit anyone to carry goods through the temple. He was teaching them: "Is it not written, My house will be called a house of prayer for all nations? But you have made it a den of thieves!" The chief priests and the scribes heard it and started looking for a way to kill him. For they were afraid of him, because the whole crowd was astonished by his teaching. Whenever evening came, they would go out of the city."

Acts 3:1 (ESV), "Now Peter and John were going up to the temple at the hour of prayer, the ninth hour."

Psalm 122:1 (CEV), "It made me glad when they said, "Let's go to the house of the LORD!"

Isaiah 2:3 (NIV), "Many peoples will come and say, "Come, let us go up to the mountain of the LORD, to the temple of the God of Jacob. He will teach us his ways, so that we may walk in his paths." The law will go out from Zion, the word of the LORD from Jerusalem."

Consider Solomon's prayer, praying for his people, the Israelite nation and even for foreigners- interceding that God would bless the temple he has built delicately with gold, precious stones and other expensive materials, and with God's permission and design given to Prophet Moses (and he was assisted with contributions from his father King David). He prayed that all who come in and seek the Lord may find answers, and all who pray towards it might find God's favour. He went into covenant with God that day. 2 Chronicles 6:18-20 (NIV), "But will God really dwell on earth with humans? The heavens, even the highest heavens, cannot contain you. How much less this temple I have built! Yet, Lord my God, give attention to your servant's prayer and his plea for mercy. Hear the cry and the prayer that your servant is praying in your presence. May your eyes be open toward this temple day and night, this place of which you said you would put your Name there. May you hear the prayer your servant prays toward this place."

Christ leaves us an example in His time of reverence for God's house, but places a call to deeper worship, not a worship of buildings but a worship of God, not a desecration of God's worship place but a honour of God's consecrated place. When Christ says "now is" it's a pointer of that present call where He points us to greater reverence of God. Not a joy of an unbeliever coming to the house of God and with no believing heart, or the trader for sales- God deserves spiritual worship; it is the believer that counts. Administrative priviledge may grant a free for all access, and family ties may cement what manner of occupation or role for maintenance, but it grieves God if they feel no true connection to the worship of God. Men builds the house, but God determines where He hallows, so it is always important that wherever His name is praised that He is truly glorified. That surely is more important. In John 4:19-26 (NLT) we see the encounter of Christ and the Samarian woman, " "Sir," the woman said, "you must be a prophet. So tell me, why is it that you Jews insist that Jerusalem is the only place of worship, while we Samaritans claim it is here at Mount Gerizim, where our ancestors worshiped?" Jesus replied, "Believe me, dear woman, the time is coming when it will no longer matter whether you worship the Father on this mountain or in Jerusalem. You Samaritans know very little about the one you worship, while we Jews know all about him, for salvation comes through the Jews. But the time is coming—indeed it's here now—when true worshipers will worship the Father in spirit and in truth. The Father is looking for those who will worship him that way. For God is Spirit, so those who worship him must worship in spirit and in truth." The woman said, "I know the Messiah is coming—the one who is called Christ. When he comes, he will explain everything to us." Then Jesus told her, "I Am the Messiah!"

Also, after ministering to a sick man (a leper), Christ had regard for the temple and those who serve in it. In Luke 1:44 (NKJV), "and said to him, "See that you say nothing to anyone; but go your way, show yourself to the priest, and offer for your cleansing those things which Moses commanded, as a testimony to them."

He also taught in the temple, Mathew 21:23-27 (ESV), "And when he entered the temple, the chief priests and the elders of the people came up to him as he was teaching, and said, "By what authority are you doing these things, and who gave you this authority?" Jesus answered them, "I also will ask you one question, and if you tell me the answer, then I also will tell you by what authority I do these things. The baptism of John, from where did it come? From heaven or from man?" And they discussed it among themselves, saying, "If we say, 'From heaven,' he will say to us, 'Why then did you not believe him?' But if we say, 'From man,' we are afraid of the crowd, for they all hold that John was a prophet." So they answered Jesus, "We do not know." And he said to them, "Neither will I tell you by what authority I do these things."

Also, Luke 2 (NLT), "Three days later they finally discovered him in the Temple, sitting among the religious teachers, listening to them and asking questions. All who heard him were amazed at his understanding and his answers. His parents didn't know what to think. "Son," his mother said to him, "why have you done this to us? Your father and I have been frantic, searching for you everywhere."

"But why did you need to search?" he asked. "Didn't you know that I must be in my Father's house?" But they didn't understand what he meant. Then he returned to Nazareth with them and was obedient to them. And his mother stored all these things in her heart. Jesus grew in wisdom and in stature and in favor with God and all the people."

I refer you to 1 Samuel 1:10-20 (NIV), Hannah would seek the Lord's face in His temple concerning her barrenness- "Once when they had finished eating and drinking in Shiloh, Hannah stood up. Now Eli the priest was sitting on his chair by the doorpost of the Lord's house. In her deep anguish Hannah prayed to the Lord, weeping bitterly. And she made a vow, saying, "Lord Almighty, if you will only look on your servant's misery and remember me, and not forget your servant but give her a son, then I will give him to the Lord for all the days of his life, and no razor will ever be used on his head." As she kept on praying to the Lord, Eli observed her mouth. Hannah was praying in her heart, and her lips were moving but her voice was not heard. Eli thought she was drunk and said to her, "How long are you going to stay drunk? Put away your wine." "Not so, my lord," Hannah replied, "I am a woman who is deeply troubled. I have not been drinking wine or beer; I was pouring out my soul to the Lord. Do not take your servant for a wicked woman; I have been praying here out of my great anguish and grief." Eli answered, "Go in peace, and may the God of Israel grant you what you have asked of him." She said, "May your servant find favor in your eyes." Then she went her way and ate something, and her face was no longer downcast. Early the next morning they arose and worshiped before the Lord and then went back to their home at Ramah. Elkanah made love to his wife Hannah, and the Lord remembered her. So in the course of time Hannah became pregnant and gave birth to a son. She named him Samuel, saying, "Because I asked the Lord for him."

Where you are not able to access the house of God because of conflict, or there is none where you are, you can have assurance that God is with you. You need not weep about inaccessibility you can trust a loving God to come to you.

See the promise of Christ in Matthew 18:20 (NIV), "For where two or three gather in my name, there am I with them."

Genesis 28:16-22 (NLT), "Then Jacob awoke from his sleep and said, "Surely the LORD is in this place, and I wasn't even aware of it!" But he was also afraid and said, "What an awesome place this is! It is none other than the house of God, the very gateway to heaven!" The next morning Jacob got up very early. He took the stone he had rested his head against, and he set it upright as a memorial pillar. Then he poured olive oil over it. He named that place Bethel (which means "house of God"), although it was previously called Luz. Then Jacob made this vow: "If God will indeed be with me and protect me on this journey, and if he will provide me with food and clothing, and if I return safely to my father's home, then the LORD will certainly be my God. And this memorial pillar I have set up will become a place for worshiping God, and I will present to God a tenth of everything he gives me." "

2 Corinthians 3:17 (NKJV), "Now the Lord is the Spirit; and where the Spirit of the Lord is, there is liberty."

Apostle Peter knew how to pray where he was. In Acts 10:9 (GNT), "The next day, as they were on their way and coming near Joppa, Peter went up on the roof of the house about noon in order to pray."

Apostle Paul would write to the Church meeting in Philemon's house, in Philemon 1:1-3.

God would deliver Daniel as he prayed in exile. He demonstrated his faith in two ways, praying openly in contradiction to King Darius's decree, and also praying towards the temple in Jerusalem since he could not go in. In Daniel 6:10-12 (NIV), "Now when Daniel learned that the decree had been published, he went home to his upstairs room where the windows opened toward Jerusalem. Three times a day he got down on his knees and prayed, giving thanks to his God, just as he had done before. Then these men went as a group and found Daniel praying and asking God for help. So they went to the king and spoke to him about his royal decree: "Did you not publish a decree that during the next thirty days anyone who prays to any god or human being except to you, Your Majesty, would be thrown into the lions' den?" The king answered, "The decree stands—in accordance with the law of the Medes and Persians, which cannot be repealed." "

It is sufficient to say, God's house is a place for reverential worship. And God would honour those who honour Him. It is God that makes a place holy. As Moses and Jacob in their different experiences understood by visitation that a place is holy ground because God is there and that His presence was made known. Christ brought to bear the teaching of His body to mean the temple, for God's presence dwells His temple. To have God's great glory in human body, is a mind-numbing thought and humbling one. Yet true- to make this happen, Christ spoke of destroying His temple (His body) and rebuilding it. A prophecy that reiterates and fulfils Prophet Joel's prophecy of God pouring His spirit on all flesh. Christ does not put an end to worship in the temple but opens our eyes to a temple not made with hands, a spiritual house made for God's glory- a place for never ending light, where God dwells with us forever in our hearts of all who trust Him.

In John 2:17-22 (NLT), "Then his disciples remembered this prophecy from the Scriptures: "Passion for God's house will consume me." But the Jewish leaders demanded, "What are you doing? If God gave you authority to do this, show us a miraculous sign to prove it." "All right," Jesus replied. "Destroy this temple, and in three days I will raise it up." "What!" they exclaimed. "It has taken forty-six years to build this Temple, and you can rebuild it in three days?" But when Jesus said "this temple," he meant his own body. After he was raised from the dead, his disciples remembered he had said this, and they believed both the Scriptures and what Jesus had said."

Ephesians 2:18-22 (ESV) tells us, "For through him we both have access in one Spirit to the Father. So then you are no longer strangers and aliens, but you are fellow citizens with the saints and members of the household of God, built on the foundation of the apostles and prophets, Christ Jesus himself being the cornerstone, in whom the whole structure, being joined together, grows into a holy temple in the Lord. In him you also are being built together into a dwelling place for God by the Spirit."

1 Corinthians 6:19-20 (GNT), "Don't you know that your body is the temple of the Holy Spirit, who lives in you and who was given to you by God? You do not belong to yourselves but to God; he bought you for a price. So use your bodies for God's glory."

When God finds His temple hallowed, both in spirit and truth, both in our lips and heart, both in our bodies inhabited by His Spirit and in a consecrated place set apart for His praise, both in His name and person- not idols made with hands, His glory will be revealed mightily in us and through us who call on the Lord of the heavens and earth.

Chapter Twenty-Five

THE SECRET PLACE OF PRAYER

- Learn to also be private in prayer, as much as possible. In the scriptures sometimes God allows us to hear some of the prayers of the patriarchs of the faith for our learning, but also we read of situations where they go to the mountain to pray, or spend quiet isolated moments with God in the temple. We have no idea of the details they said up there only the snippets revealed to us. If each of the prayers were heard, the historical writings will not contain it, and perhaps nonetheless we would still see their reliance on God for His help, the details of their fears and cry for God to reveal Himself more, and prayers for salvation as we see often in the Psalms. We must also thank God for, that some of these things where shown, because the story of their prayers has hugely encouraged many in the world who read the bible. With lots of distractions today and cameras on the roll, you may have to work twice as hard for privacy, to avoid your prayers becoming gossips and ridicule of your trust in God. Your energy must shift from distractions to a engaging more in a spiritually reflective time.

- God can hear a prayer made publicly and as well as a private prayer. The Lord however gave us an inkling into the blessedness of the secret place, even though he sometimes made sure His prayer was known, like when He prayed for the cup of suffering to pass if the Lord willed it and the disciples heard it, or about Lazarus and the people heard Him glorify God as He commanded him out from the grave; yet in Matthew 6:5-8, He tells us God hears out heartfelt prayers in our rooms too, made not for the attention of people like reading for an audience for their commendation, but as one talking to God who sees the tears, listens to the palpitation of the heart, knows the thoughts even before asking- it says this in verse 8, but is able to grant it to you. Christ was referring to the state of the heart, the need to watch against pride. To be moderate and wise in all things.

- There is amazing power in developing individual intimacy with God, knowing you will stand before God as one personally responsible for your life's choices. How about enriching your prayer life apart from when in the public arena.

- God calls us to wisdom, to being discreet. Why let those who are arrogant or faithless seek to deter your prayers because of their presumption of its' futility, and on failing to do so attempt to impeach or restrict your testimony of answers? Like Lazarus after Christ raised him from the dead, some wanted him dead again, to silence the testimony, as if to make a spoof of the moment, and create a 'proof' of Christ's non-existence or powerlessness. Who considers mental health assessment, or impact on other religions in a community, or future implications given the possibility of a person growing more powerful because of their testimony? Why not simply recognise a God moment, this man died, but a prophet of God almighty made him well? John 12:9-11 tells this clash, because, because of him many in the city were believing in Jesus Christ of Nazareth. Now I understand, why then often after a miracle Christ will say tell no one, even though He hardly could curtail their joy. It must be because He knew a miracle could open a door to jealously and other conversations for the immature (consider Luke 8:56; Mark 7:36; Luke 5:14). Why should a blessing cause more trouble to arise, and why should something of beauty and praise create divisions? It is like gold or rubies found which can bring great riches, but also attract fine thieves. So, there is caution, to not unnecessarily tell your prayers to show your plans, or shout a mistimed praise to draw an ambush to silence your testimony. But if God say pray aloud, then do so, and if your feet can't hold and you have to dance, then please do so, I am sure God delight in both your tears of pain and tears of joy. If He saved you before, He can save you twice and thrice, and if need be put a few to silence on your justification, until they learn by experience God reigns and His praise cannot be stopped eventually- even stones can sing His praise at the apportioned time.

- This also explains why the gift of tongues that enables a heavenly-kind of language, beyond supernaturally speaking in a known human language- unlearned before the time of prayer (Acts 2:5-13), as an evidence of the Holy spirit for those hearing you, can also be beneficial. Also 1 Corinthians 13:1 (NIV) says, "If I speak in the tongues of men or of angels, but do not have love, I am only a resounding gong or a clanging cymbal." God's purpose should be greater. Except God grant you grace to interpret, just keep praying and asking Him to in His discretion take control. This is because God enables you to commune in the Spirit to bring about His sovereign will with little human interference. 1 Corinthians 14:14-15 (NLT), "For if I pray in tongues, my spirit is praying, but I don't understand what I am saying. Well then, what shall I do? I will pray in the spirit, and I will also pray in words I understand. I will sing in the spirit, and I will also sing in words I understand."

Concerning the Lord, in Matthew 14:22-23 (ASV), "And straightway he constrained the disciples to enter into the boat, and to go before him unto the other side, till he should send the multitudes away. And after he had sent the multitudes away, he went up into the mountain apart to pray: and when even was come, he was there alone."

In Matthew 6:5-7 (NIV) His admonishing is, "And when you pray, do not be like the hypocrites, for they love to pray standing in the synagogues and on the street corners to be seen by others. Truly I tell you, they have received their reward in full. But when you pray, go into your room, close the door and pray to your Father, who is unseen. Then your Father, who sees what is done in secret, will reward you. And when you pray, do not keep on babbling like pagans, for they think they will be heard because of their many words."

Luke 5:16 (NIV), "But Jesus often withdrew to lonely places and prayed"

Also, in Matthew 26: 36 (NIV), "Then Jesus went with his disciples to a place called Gethsemane, and he said to them, "Sit here while I go over there and pray."

Praying with the wrong people can deflate your faith, so you may need to put them out and then talk to God- why hear mocking instead of heavenly responses that stir faith? Mark 6:5-6, tells us Christ was impeded by a people's faithlessness and could not perform miracles or do much healing. Now think of that. Limitations of the Son of God?

Consider Mark 5:35-43 (NLT), "While he was still speaking to her, messengers arrived from the home of Jairus, the leader of the synagogue. They told him, "Your daughter is dead. There's no use troubling the Teacher now." But Jesus overheard them and said to Jairus, "Don't be afraid. Just have faith." Then Jesus stopped the crowd and wouldn't let anyone go with him except Peter, James, and John (the brother of James). When they came to the home of the synagogue leader, Jesus saw much commotion and weeping and wailing. He went inside and asked, "Why all this commotion and weeping? The child isn't dead; she's only asleep." The crowd laughed at him. But he made them all leave, and he took the girl's father and mother and his three disciples into the room where the girl was lying. Holding her hand, he said to her, "Talitha koum," which means

"Little girl, get up!" And the girl, who was twelve years old, immediately stood up and walked around! They were overwhelmed and totally amazed. Jesus gave them strict orders not to tell anyone what had happened, and then he told them to give her something to eat."

Apostle Peter did the same as Christ, he put out others out of the room to pray privately, as they were very disheartened and would not help. Sometimes you need your faith exercised in a place where you have the strongest connection, a place of less doubters or very sorrowful people who will take your eyes off the Lord to only focus on their pain, but you see if you all drown in sorrow who is going to play the music to lift the mood. At some point someone has to pray, someone has to lead, someone has to sing the Lord's song- perhaps, through your faith healing and joy can flow to all that hear you and trust the Lord, and often God works through that. Acts 9:36-43 (ESV) narrates, "Now there was in Joppa a disciple named Tabitha, which, translated, means Dorcas. She was full of good works and acts of charity. In those days she became ill and died, and when they had washed her, they laid her in an upper room. Since Lydda was near Joppa, the disciples, hearing that Peter was there, sent two men to him, urging him, "Please come to us without delay." So Peter rose and went with them. And when he arrived, they took him to the upper room. All the widows stood beside him weeping and showing tunics and other garments that Dorcas made while she was with them. But Peter put them all outside, and knelt down and prayed; and turning to the body he said, "Tabitha, arise." And she opened her eyes, and when she saw Peter she sat up. And he gave her his hand and raised her up. Then, calling the saints and widows, he presented her alive. And it became known throughout all Joppa, and many believed in the Lord. And he stayed in Joppa for many days with one Simon, a tanner."

THE OPEN PLACE OF PRAYER

- Public praying is also another option for believers. Declaring the glory of God and speaking with confident assurance to a gracious God in an open space, for a testimony.

- This is about each talking to God in their public space, in their language, in their time limit, in their theme, to the hearing of those in their culture for a testimony of confidence in God. Allowing God's house erected in that environs to be a place of prayer for all who seek to pray to Jehovah. Sometimes the doors of the Church need to be open for people to come in and wait on God in prayer. Not shielded from the public, but finances needs to be set apart to allow for door security, logistics, human resources, and materials to aid praying such as the scriptures, music for worship, a sound proof cubicles if affordable, notepads for writing or drawing, lights for ambience if any need to, some light fruits or water if thirsty- at breaks. Create a place of silence and order, each in right place, attitude and prayer, not a place of trading or playful fighting and gossips. As the Holy Spirit leads. But truly some pressure or trouble may not require any of these delicate planning, just some tired knees before God and tears for help. We must however develop an attitude of prayer not only when in desperate crisis.

- Prayer is a joy, and all are welcome to enjoy and join in. If we can create a place that allows for the free flow of prayer, so God's people can go in and out in peace and wisdom borne of reverence, that would be commendable. But more importantly to carry that Spirit of prayer into our businesses, schools, government functions to pray at the opening or closure of meetings, parties and celebrations, that too has its blessing, though a relationship with the Lord is more. Also, this includes an individual taking a walk and praying in their heart, for the good of their city. This may not be every time, sometimes a walk for fresh air and to enjoy the pleasantries of creation, is just as good and delightful to God. It is a form of thanksgiving to God for life and all its beauty. Enjoy with gladness and with others. This kind of open prayer may also be done outside the church, by a group of believers as well if the Lord leads you. Like Daniel praying with the curtains open, or like the children of Israel marching around the walls of Jericho raising a thanksgiving, seeking God's triumph. You may be noticed mumbling words, or having a noticeable meditative walk as opposed to a run or joining others to lift hands and pray boldly over your city, or just sitting quietly and meditating on God's goodness, turning over every stress to God and trusting Him to take control. This is not an opportunity to judge others but to glorify God, however if you notice the distraction is too much and an avenue for persecution and temptation, then it would be best to utilise the Church space more, which also serves the public purpose but enclosed and accessible. God can still work through these, each according to their measure of faith.

In Luke 1:8-11 (ISV), "When Zechariah was serving with his division of priests in God's presence, he was chosen by lot to go into the sanctuary of the Lord and burn incense, according to the custom of the priests. And the entire congregation of people was praying outside at the time when the incense was burned. An angel of the Lord appeared to him, standing at the right side of the incense altar."

Concerning Jesus, in Luke 3:21 (ESV) "Now when all the people were baptized, and when Jesus also had been baptized and was praying, the heavens were opened, and the Holy Spirit descended on him in bodily form, like a dove; and a voice came from heaven, "You are my beloved Son; with you I am well pleased.""

Sometimes rather than pray alone- withdrawing to a lonely space, you may need to pray in public, take or join a group of people, or perhaps circumstance may require you can only pray with the immediate others around you. This can also be effective, and you can anticipate the affirming glory of God. I perceive God allows this because it can be an opportunity for the glory of God to be revealed as a testimony, so those present can see God at work. This is because, say when praying alone and God visits you or sends an Angel, or something strange happens, some will not believe your story, but when God does something out of the natural and others see, it becomes a food for thought, a testimony for those who believe that God is there and hears, and with you. Or say someone knows about your problem, and later hear of a solution- they go really, I knew of that, how?! When you pray in a group, make sure you participate, not just observe (Luke 9:18). A prayer in agreement is important, but one who fears God may truly only be the one praying if others there are complacent, playing with words, or perhaps not mature yet. So, do not play along, pray along. If still a child, a parent may take you along, so when you grow you may find the lessons helpful, so important to be unjudgmental and give grace for growth.

Luke 9:28 (ESV) tells us this incident with Christ, "Now about eight days after these sayings he took with him Peter and John and James and went up on the mountain to pray. And as he was praying, the appearance of his face was altered, and his clothing became dazzling white. And behold, two men were talking with him, Moses and Elijah, who appeared in glory and spoke of his departure, which he was about to accomplish at Jerusalem. Now Peter and those who were with him were heavy with sleep, but when they became fully awake they saw his glory and the two men who stood with him. And as the men were parting from him, Peter said to Jesus, "Master, it is good that we are here. Let us make three tents, one for you and one for Moses and one for Elijah"—not knowing what he said. As he was saying these things, a cloud came and overshadowed them, and they were afraid as they entered the cloud. And a voice came out of the cloud, saying, "This is my Son, my Chosen One; listen to him!" And when the voice had spoken, Jesus was found alone. And they kept silent and told no one in those days anything of what they had seen."

Consider Acts 12:5-11 (NIV), "So Peter was kept in prison, but the church was earnestly praying to God for him. The night before Herod was to bring him to trial, Peter was sleeping between two soldiers, bound with two chains, and sentries stood guard at the entrance. Suddenly an angel of the Lord appeared and a light shone in the cell. He struck Peter on the side and woke him up. "Quick, get up!" he said, and the chains fell off Peter's wrists. Then the angel said to him, "Put on your clothes and sandals." And Peter did so. "Wrap your cloak around you and follow me," the angel told him. Peter followed him out of the prison, but he had no idea that what the angel was doing was really happening; he thought he was seeing a vision. They passed the first and second guards and came to the iron gate leading to the city. It opened for them by itself, and they went through it. When they had walked the length of one street, suddenly the angel left him. Then Peter came to himself and said, "Now I know without a doubt that the Lord has sent his angel and rescued me from Herod's clutches and from everything the Jewish people were hoping would happen.""

Chapter Twenty-Seven

THE MEMORABLE PLACE OF PRAYER

- The memorable place is where God turned up. A moment God showed up. You may want to recognise that it was in that place you sought the Lord. Nothing overly emotional, it means whilst you prayed you recalled not only what you said, but where you where, and what God said to you or encountered Him in a unique way. Most unusual encounters with God are memorable.

- It could also be the place where you first conversed with God on a subject matter, and had an answer subsequently, a deep sense that something out of the ordinary occurred or relief it is now taken care of.

God hears prayers but also remembers. He has a good memory. You can be sure each word said is important and recorded in His book. If God remembers you and answers, remember your testimony- teach it your children and others who will listen of His faithfulness.

Psalm 20:3-4 (NIV) says, "May he remember all your sacrifices and accept your burnt offerings. May he give you the desire of your heart and make all your plans succeed."

In Acts 10:4 (NIV), "One day at about three in the afternoon he had a vision. He distinctly saw an angel of God, who came to him and said, "Cornelius!" Cornelius stared at him in fear. "What is it, Lord?" he asked. The angel answered, "Your prayers and gifts to the poor have come up as a memorial offering before God."

Christ did not rebuke Apostle Peter when He talked about asking Moses and Elijah to stay in the vision they saw whilst with Jesus; the vision was so glorious as Christ commune with the Lord- they saw the need to not let the moment go. God will say you have Christ with you, listen to Him. Thank God for the priviledge of the testimony but remember to continue with the Lord.

Matthew 17:3-4 (NKJV), "And behold, Moses and Elijah appeared to them, talking with Him. Then Peter answered and said to Jesus, "Lord, it is good for us to be here; if You wish, let us make here three tabernacles: one for You, one for Moses, and one for Elijah.""

There is something about placing a memorable mark where God delivered you- saying, here, in this place, at this precious time, in this circumstance, God gave me or us deliverance, and then passing that story or physical signage on. The significance is for others to see, learn, and fear the Lord.

Consider 1 Samuel 7:9-13 (GWT), "Then Samuel took a lamb, one still feeding on milk, and sacrificed it as a burnt offering to the LORD. Samuel cried to the LORD on behalf of Israel, and the LORD answered him. While Samuel was sacrificing the burnt offering, the Philistines came to fight against Israel. On that day the LORD thundered loudly at the Philistines and threw them into such confusion that they were defeated by Israel. Israel's soldiers left Mizpah, pursued the Philistines, and killed them as far as Beth Car. Then Samuel took a rock and set it up between Mizpah and Shen. He named it Ebenezer [Rock of Help] and said, "Until now the LORD has helped us." The power of the Philistines was crushed, so they didn't come into Israel's territory again. The LORD restrained the Philistines as long as Samuel lived." (Genesis 28:18-22)

Deuteronomy 11:16-21 (NIV) (see also verses 2-7), "Be careful, or you will be enticed to turn away and worship other gods and bow down to them. Then the LORD's anger will burn against you, and he will shut up the heavens so that it will not rain and the ground will yield no produce, and you will soon perish from the good land the LORD is giving you. Fix these words of mine in your hearts and minds; tie them as symbols on your hands and bind them on your foreheads. Teach them to your children, talking about them when you sit at home and when you walk along the road, when you lie down and when you get up. Write them on the doorframes of your houses and on your gates, so that your days and the days of your children may be many in the land the LORD swore to give your ancestors, as many as the days that the heavens are above the earth."

I refer you to 1 Corinthians 11:23-26 (NKJV) where Christ commands us to commit to actively be in memory of Him and what He has done for us in this world who trust Him, an answer to the plea for spiritual deliverance from the power of satan through His death on the cross, as we on the Lord's day take the bread and wine, "For I received from the Lord that which I also delivered to you: that the Lord Jesus on the same night in which He was betrayed took bread; and when He had given thanks, He broke it and said, "Take, eat; this is My body which is broken for you; do this in remembrance of Me." In the same manner He also took the cup after supper, saying, "This cup is the new covenant in My blood. This do, as often as you drink it, in remembrance of Me." For as often as you eat this bread and drink this cup, you proclaim the Lord's death till He comes."

Chapter Twenty-Eight

THE ACTIONS OF PRAYER

- Prayer is action, its active and potent. It is not a passive or an undesired option, it is tangible. Prayer requires time, some mental and physical commitment.

- The bible refers to the acts of the Apostles, their spiritual activity as a continuum, as an engagement of practice and discipline. It takes tenacity and patience to wait on the Lord.

The Apostles for instance saw the need to make more effort at making a deliberate administrative plan to pray, as in those days as division arose in the Church, in response they appointed leaders to oversee hospitality in the Church to foster unity, whilst they created more time for prayer- Acts 6:2-4 (GWT), "The twelve apostles called all the disciples together and told them, "It's not right for us to give up God's word in order to distribute food. So, brothers and sisters, choose seven men whom the people know are spiritually wise. We will put them in charge of this problem. However, we will devote ourselves to praying and to serving in ways that are related to the word.""

The Lord's labour in prayer brought great sweat to His body- consider the intensity of His plea on His knees, in Luke 22:44-46 (GNT) "In great anguish he prayed even more fervently; his sweat was like drops of blood falling to the ground. Rising from his prayer, he went back to the disciples and found them asleep, worn out by their grief. He said to them, "Why are you sleeping? Get up and pray that you will not fall into temptation."

Luke 6:12 (ERV), "And it came to pass in these days, that he went out into the mountain to pray; and he continued all night in prayer to God."

Apostle Paul in Colossians 4:12 (ISV) writes of, "Epaphras, who is one of you, a servant of the Messiah Jesus, sends you his greetings. He is always wrestling in his prayers for you, so that you may stand mature, completely convinced of the entire will of God."

Consider the steps of Prophet Moses in prayer, the effort, the days spent alone with God- Exodus 24:12-16 (ESV), "The Lord said to Moses, "Come up to me on the mountain and wait there, that I may give you the tablets of stone, with the law and the commandment, which I have written for their instruction." So Moses rose with his assistant Joshua, and Moses went up into the mountain of God. And he said to the elders, "Wait here for us until we return to you. And behold, Aaron and Hur are with you. Whoever has a dispute, let him go to them." Then Moses went up on the mountain, and the cloud covered the mountain. The glory of the Lord dwelt on Mount Sinai, and the cloud covered it six days. And on the seventh day he called to Moses out of the midst of the cloud. Now the appearance of the glory of the Lord was like a devouring fire on the top of the mountain in the sight of the people of Israel. Moses entered the cloud and went up on the mountain. And Moses was on the mountain forty days and forty nights."

Prayer could put considerable strain on the body. It requires effective time management, side-lining distractions, concentration, mental strength and discipline. It is more than just a talk to an invisible being, but an invisible being who is creator God, of the heavens and earth, requiring a belief in His abilities as you present your case, committing your energies according to your abilities to persuade Him of your needs. Often the trial each face may determine the level of strain on emotions but remember each time

God is with you and sees your difficulties. But take that step to pray trusting Him for answers.

Chapter Twenty-Nine

PRAYER AND OBEDIENCE

- Obedience makes us pray. It is God's instruction to listen to His words, counsel, and do them, and one of which is to talk to Him about our cares and worship Him in thanksgiving.

- Obedience to God in prayer is not only fulfilling the obligation but also praying out His good purpose. You cannot rightfully pray for power to be disobedient, and you cannot contemplate a vibrant relationship with God void of conversation with Him. It is an opportunity for an open heaven to God's blessings. It is true to say obedience would attract heaven's attention.

Isaiah 1:19-20 (AMP) says, " "Come now, and let us reason together," Says the Lord. "Though your sins are like scarlet, They shall be as white as snow; Though they are red like crimson, They shall be like wool. "If you are willing and obedient, You shall eat the best of the land; But if you refuse and rebel, You shall be devoured by the sword." For the mouth of the Lord has spoken."

Also, Jeremiah 29:12-14 (NIV), "Then you will call on me and come and pray to me, and I will listen to you. You will seek me and find me when you seek me with all your heart. I will be found by you," declares the Lord, "and will bring you back from captivity. I will gather you from all the nations and places where I have banished you," declares the Lord, "and will bring you back to the place from which I carried you into exile."'"

In Deuteronomy 27:9-10 (CEV), "Moses stood together with the priests and said, "Israel, be quiet and listen to me! Today you have become the people of the Lord your God. So you must obey his laws and teachings that I am giving you."

Proverbs 4:20-27 (NIV), "My son, pay attention to what I say; turn your ear to my words. Do not let them out of your sight, keep them within your heart; for they are life to those who find them and health to one's whole body. Above all else, guard your heart, for everything you do flows from it. Keep your mouth free of perversity; keep corrupt talk far from your lips. Let your eyes look straight ahead; fix your gaze directly before you. Give careful thought to the paths for your feet and be steadfast in all your ways. Do not turn to the right or the left; keep your foot from evil."

Deuteronomy 6:13-14 (CEV), "Worship and obey the Lord your God with fear and trembling, and promise that you will be loyal to him. Don't have anything to do with gods that are worshiped by the nations around you."

On one hand, obedience fulfils the call to pray, and you do well in that, but disobedience in our lifestyle could impede God's positive response in answering or enabling the best outcome for your request. Wisdom then is to walk wisely in complete obedience, so your prayers are not hindered. I have an obligation to enrich your faith by sharing this truth with you. God assures us who rely on Him of His perfect and overflowing mercy (Psalm 103:17; Luke 1:49-50; Romans 9:14-33). As you stand in Christ's righteousness, putting on His garment, we all who believe can come into God's purpose in Christ's name.

Proverbs 14:34-35 (ISV), "Righteousness makes a nation great, but sin diminishes any people. The king approves the wise servant, but he is angry at anyone who acts shamefully."

Isaiah 59:1-4 (GNT) says, "Don't think that the Lord is too weak to save you or too deaf to hear your call for help! It is because of your sins that he doesn't hear you. It is your sins that separate you from God when you try to worship him. You are guilty of lying, violence, and murder. You go to court, but you do not have justice on your side. You depend on lies to win your case. You carry out your plans to hurt others."

Chapter Thirty

IGNORE COUNTERFEIT PRAYER

- Important to learn to discern counterfeit answers and counterfeit prayers, from a Christ inspired prayer and God-given answers. And then move to binding a critic-hypocritical and envious spirit.

- A feature of prayers that run counter to the good purpose of God is one oriented around self and running contrary to the mind of the Spirit.

- God gives good gifts, so avoid Satan's games or antics that lead to bitterness towards one another, or that discourages your open-hearted prayers.

There are those who wonder why the wicked who pray deceitfully continue gaining ground, surviving by deceit and cunningness, prospering in their ways, even mocking God and getting away with it- until the Psalmist in 73rd chapter caught a glimpse of the intellect of God, that the end of the game was paramount with God. God had designed that they be deceived by their own deception, and that even if they seemed to have solutions, He allows it as a slippery slope to take them into destructive oblivion. In all, mocking God will not produce true progress.

I refer you to these verses, Psalm 73:12-17 (NLT), "Look at these wicked people— enjoying a life of ease while their riches multiply. Did I keep my heart pure for nothing? Did I keep myself innocent for no reason? I get nothing but trouble all day long; every morning brings me pain. If I had really spoken this way to others, I would have been a traitor to your people. So I tried to understand why the wicked prosper. But what a difficult task it is! Then I went into your sanctuary, O God, and I finally understood the destiny of the wicked."

Don't pray to other gods, made after the representation of human imaginations, animal creatures, or likeness of humans. These man-made gods are not the living God, God almighty is the creator of the heavens and the earth, and His name is Jehovah. Christ calls Him Father. And the Lord Jesus of Nazareth, the Christ, proceeds from the Father, and is one with the Spirit of God. He warns us there is none beside Him. God is the I am, that I am. And He is glorified in His Son and is named in Him. And, Christ promises in His name, God's authority is also revealed. Revealed to heal, bless, provide, defend, uplift, redeem, and to command all the blessings of heaven.

Consider Exodus 20 (NIV), ""You shall have no other gods before me. "You shall not make for yourself an image in the form of anything in heaven above or on the earth beneath or in the waters below. You shall not bow down to them or worship them; for I, the Lord your God, am a jealous God, punishing the children for the sin of the parents to the third and fourth generation of those who hate me, but showing love to a thousand generations of those who love me and keep my commandments. "You shall not misuse the name of the Lord your God, for the Lord will not hold anyone guiltless who misuses his name."

In Matthew 4:5-7 (NLT) we are reminded that it is in rightly applying the scriptures that bring results- "Then the devil took him to the holy city, Jerusalem, to the highest point of the Temple, and said, "If you are the Son of God, jump off! For the Scriptures say, 'He will order his angels to protect you. And they will hold you up with their hands so you won't even hurt your foot on a stone.'" Jesus responded, "The Scriptures also say, 'You must not test the Lord your God.'"

The story in 1 Kings 13, is a helpful guide in discerning prayers and answers. In this case two Prophets had conflicting revelations, the older Prophet asked the younger one to discountenance a divine instruction not to have a meal at his house because he had a different spiritual response from God, which led to his demise. See the depth of the deceit in God's name, yet God will not excuse that- Verses 15-19 of that chapter says, "So the prophet said to him, "Come home with me and eat." The man of God said, "I cannot turn back and go with you, nor can I eat bread or drink water with you in this place. I have been told by the word of the Lord: 'You must not eat bread or drink water there or return by the way you came.'" The old prophet answered, "I too am a prophet, as you are. And an angel said to me by the word of the Lord: 'Bring him back with you to your house so that he may eat bread and drink water.'" (But he was lying to him.) So the man of God returned with him and ate and drank in his house."

This cautions God's people not to be led to pray in a direction that achieves a purpose if God is not in it, or to follow an instruction not from God, or say amen to a thus says the Lord when it's not the Lord. Some prayers can be misleading and some supposed answers from God can equally be wrong- so do not let another deceive you.

Chapter Thirty-One

THE SPIRIT OF PRAYER, AND THE JOY OF FELLOWSHIP WITH THE HOLY SPIRIT

- By the Spirit of prayer, I mean being open to the spontaneity and promptings of the Spirit.

- It is a joyful priviledge to pray before the presence of a great God and His Spirit.

Here we see the father heart of God, for joyful communion. We find joy in praying, but also trust that through our prayer God can make us enjoy joyful living, within one's heart and with others. As you talk to God the overwhelming feeling of peace and joy flows from God's spirit, learn to recognise and accept it, let it stay on you don't hold back the feeling, its more that adrenaline, that is God reaching for you.

In Isaiah 56:7 (NIV) "these I will bring to my holy mountain and give them joy in my house of prayer. Their burnt offerings and sacrifices will be accepted on my altar; for my house will be called a house of prayer for all nations."

Acts 2:42 (NLT), shows us- "All the believers devoted themselves to the apostles' teaching, and to fellowship, and to sharing in meals (including the Lord's Supper), and to prayer."

The lonely, widowed, can find comfort and fellowship with the Lord in prayer (Luke 2:37). Also 1 Timothy 5:5 (NIV) says, "The widow who is really in need and left all alone puts her hope in God and continues night and day to pray and to ask God for help."

Prayer do not replace physical company of a beloved one, or Christian fellowship together, but it's a means God uses to enhance our fellowship together as believers, as we can pray for each other and look forward to developing that godly affection for their wellbeing as well.

Apostle Paul would write in 2 Timothy 1:3-4 (NLT), "Timothy, I thank God for you—the God I serve with a clear conscience, just as my ancestors did. Night and day I constantly remember you in my prayers. I long to see you again, for I remember your tears as we parted. And I will be filled with joy when we are together again." (Philemon 1:4-7)

1 Thessalonians 3:6-13 (NIV) Apostle Paul's letter to the Thessalonians would also reveal this interesting web of prayer, encouragement, thanksgiving – of a loving Christian fellowship which the Holy Spirit had enabled in the Church; "But Timothy has just now come to us from you and has brought good news about your faith and love. He has told us that you always have pleasant memories of us and that you long to see us, just as we also long to see you. Therefore, brothers and sisters, in all our distress and persecution we were encouraged about you because of your faith. For now we really live, since you are standing firm in the Lord. How can we thank God enough for you in return for all the joy we have in the presence of our God because of you? Night and day we pray most earnestly that we may see you again and supply what is lacking in your faith. Now may our God and Father himself and our Lord Jesus clear the way for us to come to you. May the Lord make your love increase and overflow for each other and for everyone else, just as ours does for you. May he strengthen your hearts so that you will be blameless and holy in the presence of our God and Father when our Lord Jesus comes with all his holy ones."

Consider this encouragement in Jude 1:17-21 (NIV), "But, dear friends, remember what the apostles of our Lord Jesus Christ foretold. They said to you, "In the last times there will be scoffers who will follow their own ungodly desires." These are the people who divide you, who follow mere natural instincts and do not have the Spirit. But you, dear friends, by building yourselves up in your most holy faith and praying in the Holy Spirit, keep yourselves in God's love as you wait for the mercy of our Lord Jesus Christ to bring you to eternal life."

Romans 8:26-27 (GNT), tells us further that the Holy Spirit would assist our praying, so we can pray right and build our intimacy with God, and have His love flow through us- "In the same way the Spirit also comes to help us, weak as we are. For we do not know how we ought to pray; the Spirit himself pleads with God for us in groans that words cannot express. And God, who sees into our hearts, knows what the thought of the Spirit is; because the Spirit pleads with God on behalf of his people and in accordance with his will."

Chapter Thirty-Two

PRAYING THE SCRIPTURES

- The bible gives us examples of prayers by some renown people, that moved the heart of God. Consider for example some of David's prayers of thanksgiving, Solomon's prayer of dedication of the temple, the prayer of Christ as He taught His disciples and His prayers in other circumstances, Apostle Paul's prayers for the Churches he wrote to, the Psalms, and so on. These examples can help young believers in their mastery of prayer.

These prayers in the bible may be recited in faith as it applies to your circumstance, as God leads you. For example the Lord's prayer in Matthew 6 progresses from a reverence for God, acknowledging Him as father and recognising His place, "in heaven", and then to an invitation for Him to dwell in the midst of us and ruling by His triumphant will. It also features a request for needs to be met but also a commitment to be merciful, as we look to the mercy of God for deliverance from the snare of Satan, so he does not gain a foothold. This blueprint, of encompassing prayer of thanks, a submission to divine will, request, plea, intercession, deliverance, is still relevant today.

You can also feel free to be expressive and expand this prayer to fit your individual stories or cases, and talk to God about it, if you are gifted to do so. We see situations as I have shown earlier, of Kings in the bible talking to God specifically about their fears and threats of their enemy, of prophets speaking to God for deliverance and direction, of women and men praying for their families calling to God. Also, in the bible as you search you will find the promises of God, which you can affirm them over your life and also present your reasons as Prophet Isaiah said, before God, and then ask Him humbly to hear you. As Christ suggests, go indoors, shut your doors from distractions, kneel before God and pour your heart to Him. God who hears in secret, will reward you openly. To handle a troubling situation, you may take whatever lawful but godly action necessary, and keep praying to God about it, according to the word, ask Him to fulfil His word and magnify His name in you.

For example consider praying Matthew 6:9-13 (1 Kings 8:22-53; Psalm 23; John 11:41-42; Acts 4:23-31)-

"This, then, is how you should pray:
"Our Father in heaven,
hallowed be your name,
your kingdom come,
your will be done,
on earth as it is in heaven.
Give us today our daily bread.
And forgive us our debts,
as we also have forgiven our debtors.
And lead us not into temptation,
but deliver us from the evil one."

Also, consider praying Psalm 71-

"In You, O Lord, I put my trust;
Let me never be put to shame.
Deliver me in Your righteousness, and cause me to escape;
Incline Your ear to me, and save me.
Be my strong refuge,

To which I may resort continually;
You have given the commandment to save me,
For You are my rock and my fortress.
Deliver me, O my God, out of the hand of the wicked,
Out of the hand of the unrighteous and cruel man.
For You are my hope, O Lord God;
You are my trust from my youth.
By You I have been upheld from birth;
You are He who took me out of my mother's womb.
My praise shall be continually of You.
I have become as a wonder to many,
But You are my strong refuge.
Let my mouth be filled with Your praise
And with Your glory all the day.
Do not cast me off in the time of old age;
Do not forsake me when my strength fails.
For my enemies speak against me;
And those who lie in wait for my life take counsel together,
Saying, "God has forsaken him;
Pursue and take him, for there is none to deliver him."
O God, do not be far from me;
O my God, make haste to help me!
Let them be confounded and consumed
Who are adversaries of my life;
Let them be covered with reproach and dishonor
Who seek my hurt.
But I will hope continually,
And will praise You yet more and more.
My mouth shall tell of Your righteousness
And Your salvation all the day,
For I do not know their limits.
I will go in the strength of the Lord God;
I will make mention of Your righteousness, of Yours only.
O God, You have taught me from my youth;

And to this day I declare Your wondrous works.
Now also when I am old and grayheaded,
O God, do not forsake me,
Until I declare Your strength to this generation,
Your power to everyone who is to come.
Also Your righteousness, O God, is very high,
You who have done great things;
O God, who is like You?
You, who have shown me great and severe troubles,
Shall revive me again,
And bring me up again from the depths of the earth.
You shall increase my greatness,
And comfort me on every side.
Also with the lute I will praise You—
And Your faithfulness, O my God!
To You I will sing with the harp,
O Holy One of Israel.
My lips shall greatly rejoice when I sing to You,
And my soul, which You have redeemed.
My tongue also shall talk of Your righteousness all the day long;
For they are confounded,
For they are brought to shame
Who seek my hurt."

Amen.

Chapter Thirty-Three

HIGHER DIMENSIONS OF PRAYER: HEAVEN'S PRE-EMPTIVE GRACE

- There is something beautiful about receiving before asking, which is almost an exception to the natural progression of a spiritual principle of prayer based on request. This is true when from a heart in tune with one's maker. So, request is emanating from His will, and it is when there is grace for priviledge such that God makes haste to pre-empt and fulfil a need before even labouring in prayers.

- Isn't it incredible to receive answers whilst your request is still in your thoughts? Or better still to get an answer and then recognise this was what you needed all the while, and then wonder why you forgot to ask for it. That is God, He gives what you need, even that which is beyond your capacity to ask for each moment.

Isaiah 65:24 (NLT) says, "I will answer them before they even call to me. While they are still talking about their needs, I will go ahead and answer their prayers!"

Psalm 37:4 (NLT), "Take delight in the LORD, and he will give you your heart's desires."

Daniel 10:12 (AMP), "Then he said to me, "Do not be afraid, Daniel, for from the first day that you set your heart on understanding this and on humbling yourself before your God, your words were heard, and I have come in response to your words."

Genesis 18:17-18 (NIV), "Then the Lord said, "Shall I hide from Abraham what I am about to do? Abraham will surely become a great and powerful nation, and all nations on earth will be blessed through him."

The key is to set your heart right, and then come to the place of prayer. You will be surprised to realise God saw the start point to the finish point of your prayer, that is from the moment you contemplated praying to the conclusion. And like Daniel, his answer came from the moment he set his heart to understand and humble himself before God. Have you met someone who you tried to explain how to bake a cake, and they say, "don't bother." I am sure if you persist, they probably will not be interested to hear, and you may not be stimulated to explain either. But a set heart to receive changes the mood and plan, which is a proper state. If ready, you might say, "okay, we meet at Twins Crossway, at two pm in the afternoon, and head straight to a Café for a conversation. So, come with a notepad." Similarly, God's answers are often predicated on a prepared heart, a lip of godly understanding, of what the will of God is and purpose, and an openness to the timing and discretion of God.

Author's Biography Page

Israel Chukwuka Okunwaye, Dip.sc (Benin), LL. B (Benin), BL (Lagos), LLM (Birmingham), M.A (Birmingham)

Author and Christian Speaker
Founder, Glyglobal.

Israel Chukwuka Okunwaye is a Christian Evangelist and minister of the gospel of Jesus Christ, called of God and with a heart to reach all people with the love that there is in Christ. For many years, now turning into decades he has been communicating this message of the Cross at the grassroots and also on several platforms with the fervour it demands, and with the tremendous spiritual grace the Lord supplies. He has had the priviledge to work secularly, and has tackled some pressing social issues. He has written several works including these books, *Authentic Faith, The Heart of Passion, Rethinking Leadership,* and *Prayer Intelligence.* He believes that it is in the loving arms of God you will find all the answers you need. He is the founder of www.glyglobal.com, an online evangelistic network and outreach with free access to credible Christian faith resource and information, which has morphed into an instrumental tool in reaching many with the gospel across the nations [Glyglobal®], since the first launch many years ago. As a visionary, leader, and anointed speaker, he is graced to teach and minister the word with clarity, and prophetic unction. He also worked briefly as a human rights lawyer in Nigeria and is a staunch advocate for principles of social justice; and is concerned about the plight of the disadvantaged and affirm causes in aid. He believes that the call to Christian living should also drive social action.

He has been priviledged to lead a university campus Christian fellowship with Pentecostal roots, affiliated to Christ's Chosen Church of God Int'l, for some years as President, and thereafter as National President; and was involved in the University of Benin's Christian Community on Campus executive as the Public Relations Officer, a worthy cause of galvanising the body of Christ towards spiritual goals. Prior to this he has been involved with the Scripture Union locally, in encouraging young people and facilitating meetings. In Abuja– Nigeria, he led the work as Evangelism Coordinator under the auspices of the Nigeria Christian Corpers' Fellowship to mobilise efforts at reaching city dwellers and especially those in the rural areas with the gospel, and with practical relief support. Also, working alongside the team at an Elim Pentecostal Church in Selly Oak, Birmingham– UK as Evangelical worker led reaching out to the community and stirred the Church towards soul winning. As one with an evangelistic grace and zeal to see the frontiers for the gospel expand, he has been enabled to serve as Chaplain with CIGB UK [Churches and Industry Group Birmingham and Solihull] with a mission to minister to people at the workplace. He believes in the body of Christ being missional in the community where placed and has organised bible studies to explore and understand the Christian message in response to questions of faith; he continues to be at the forefront of teaching and conveying the word, through his resources, projects, and on speaking platforms. He identifies with the Evangelical Alliance UK as a member. Evangelist Israel, hold in affirmation the foundational doctrines of faith along with fellow believers, and the Apostles' Creed. He has attended the International Bible Institute of London [IBIOL], Kensington Temple, London, studying the course on Apologetics, and also a Church based ministry training programme,

Midlands Ministry Training Course [MMTC], at the Midlands Gospel Partnership, Birmingham.

He is a M.A graduate of the School of Philosophy, Theology and Religion, of University of Birmingham, and has an LLM from the Birmingham Law School. He has also received a BL from the Nigeria Law School, Lagos, after completing his bachelor's degree with the University of Benin.

For further information on ministry update and contact– www.israelokunwaye.com.

www.ingramcontent.com/pod-product-compliance
Lightning Source LLC
Chambersburg PA
CBHW032000080426
42735CB00007B/457